JERUSALEM TO ROME

Studies in the Book of Acts

JERUSALEM TO ROME
Studies in the Book of Acts

by

Homer A. Kent, Jr.

BAKER BOOK HOUSE
Grand Rapids, Michigan

Library of Congress Catalog Card Number: 77-187723

ISBN: 0-8010-5313-7

Copyright, 1972, by
Brethren Missionary Herald

Baker Book House and BMH Books co-publishers

PRINTED IN THE UNITED STATES OF AMERICA

To KATHY
in loving gratitude for her lively spirit,
her interest in God's Word,
and the joy that is mine just by being her father

ACKNOWLEDGMENTS

The contributions of many have been utilized in the producing of this volume. In addition to the students at Grace Theological Seminary who through twenty-one years have been studying Acts with the writer and have helped to refine the material herewith presented, the following individuals merit special mention:

Mr. Robert D. Ibach, Jr., who labored with diligence and great skill in preparing the maps, charts, and the temple diagram.

Dr. James L. Boyer, who graciously granted to the author the privilege of using portions of his New Testament Chronological Chart, and who read the manuscript and gave valuable suggestions.

Dr. and Mrs. Homer A. Kent, Sr., the author's parents, who also read the manuscript and made helpful suggestions.

Mr. Arthur W. Davis, who prepared the cover.

To all of these, as well as to the many authors of today and yesterday whose writings have contributed greatly to his understanding of the Book of Acts, the writer acknowledges his profound debt and deep gratitude.

CONTENTS

LIST OF ILLUSTRATIONS

Photo Credits

Fratelli Alinari, Instituto Di Edizioni Artistiche, Via Nazionale, 6, Florence, Italy.
Israel Department of Antiquities and Museums, Ministry of Education and Culture, P. O. B. 586, Jerusalem, Israel.
Levant Photo Service, P. O. Box 1284, Santa Cruz, California, 95060.
Ministere des Affaires Culturelles, Palais du Louvre, Paris 1er, France, 488.59.40.
Palphot Limited, P. O. B. 2, Herzlia, Israel.
Photographs not otherwise credited are by the author.

TRANSLITERATION

Whenever possible, Hebrew and Greek words have been transliterated according to the following form:

Greek	Consonants	Vocalization
a — a	א — '	— ā
ϵ — e	ב — b, b̲	— a
η — ē	ג — g, g̲	— e
o — o	ד — d, d̲	— ē
ω — ō	ה — h	— ê
ζ — z	ו — w	— i
θ — th	ז — z	— î
ξ — x	ח — ḥ	— ŏ
υ — u	ט — ṭ	— o
ϕ — ph	י — y	— û
χ — ch	כ — k, k̲	— u
ψ — ps	ל — l	— ( )e
— h	מ — m	
$\dot{\rho}$ — rh	נ — n	
α — āi	ס — s	
η — ēi	ע — '	
ω — ōi	פ — p, p̲	
$\gamma\gamma$ — ng	צ — ṣ	
$\gamma\kappa$ — nk	ק — q	
$\gamma\xi$ — nx	ר — r	
$\gamma\chi$ — nch	שׂ — ś	
	שׁ — š	
	ת — t, t̲	

ABBREVIATIONS

Arndt-Gingrich	*A Greek-English Lexicon of the New Testament*
ASV	American Standard Version, 1901
Bible Societies Text	Greek NT published by the United Bible Societies, 1966
KJV	King James Version, 1611
LXX	Septuagint (Greek translation of the OT)
NASB	New American Standard Bible, 1971
NEB	New English Bible, 1961
NT	New Testament
OT	Old Testament
RSV	Revised Standard Version, 1952
TDNT	*Theological Dictionary of the NT*

PREFACE

The Book of Acts becomes more fascinating the more one studies it. Its pages provide the only reliable account of what really happened between the ascension of Jesus Christ and the remarkable spread of the Christian faith. It is the vital link between the earthly life of Christ which began and ended in Judea, and the Christian church which by the middle of the first century was to be found among gentiles as well as Jews as far away as Rome, and in most of the major centers in between.

The writer's aim in this little volume is to place the thrilling story of Acts against its historical background. Only then can its import be fully appreciated. Limitations of space have prevented a verse-by-verse treatment, but the grand movement of the gospel has been traced with careful attention given to its crucial moments. The reader will profit most from these studies if each section is read with Bible in hand.

After twenty-one years of teaching the Book of Acts annually to students at Grace Theological Seminary, the writer continues to contemplate its message with excitement. It is his devout hope that those who use this volume may find their understanding deepened and their faith increased, and that they may joyfully and proudly join with Paul as he spoke of his Lord in words of personal commitment, "Whose I am and whom I serve" (Acts 27:23).

Homer A. Kent, Jr.

Winona Lake, Indiana

INTRODUCTION

The Book of Acts occupies a pivotal spot in the New Testament, and must have served a vital function in the early church. It was written to a man named Theophilus, a person not otherwise known to us, but one who had received basic instruction in the life of Jesus Christ from Luke's Gospel (1:4). His experience was doubtless characteristic of many who had come into contact with the Christian movement. As they did so, they would have been confronted with institutional churches, organized groups of believers in various cities who met regularly for prayer, instruction, fellowship, and observance of the ordinances. They would have become acquainted with officials such as elders and deacons (Phil. 1:1), with established procedures for caring for widows (I Tim. 5:3-16) and disciplining their members (I Cor. 5:3-5), and Jews and gentiles joined together on completely equal terms — not through proselytization but by virtue of their common faith in Christ which brought the regeneration that had formed them into one spiritual body.

When those early converts asked how it all came about, they would have been directed to the incomparable story of Jesus Christ, his life, his teachings, and his sacrificial death and resurrection. At first this story was told by word of mouth; later it became enshrined in the four written Gospels. Yet there would remain some unanswered questions. One does not find the institutional church in the life of Jesus. There are no Christian elders or deacons in the Gospels. The free association of Jews and gentiles, part being circumcised and part not, has no explanation in the career of Jesus. The wholesale proclamation of the gospel to gentiles is not to be traced to the earthly example of Jesus, except by anticipation in the final commission given by him to his disciples. How does it happen that Christianity as seen by men like Theophilus took the form which it did, quite different in some respects from its Gospel origins?

The Book of Acts bridges this gap. It answers these questions

13

not only for Theophilus, but also for every sincere reader who
devotes himself seriously to its message. Its position in the NT,
after the Gospels and before the Epistles, is thus a logical one,
for Acts shows how the Christian movement, based upon Christ's
redemptive work as depicted in the Gospel accounts, expanded
from its Palestinian origins to the heart of the gentile world.
Acts provides also a necessary background for understanding
the Epistles. Until one is familiar with Acts he really cannot
comprehend the circumstances which caused the Epistles to
be written. To this remarkable book the reader is invited to
give his careful attention that he may learn the story of Christian beginnings.

Author

No author is named specifically in Acts, although the work
has been attributed to Luke as far back as we can trace. As early
as the second century records exist which state that he wrote
both the third Gospel and Acts. The earliest witness to Luke's
authorship is the Anti-Marcionite Prologue to Luke, dated
around A.D. 150-180, which also gives it the title "The Acts of
the Apostles." Other early sources which agree on Lukan
authorship are the Muratorian Canon, Irenaeus, Clement of
Alexandria, and Tertullian. There is no conflicting tradition
during this period. This is strong evidence, for Luke is otherwise an almost unknown figure, and there would be no *a priori*
reason to attribute authorship to him.

From Acts itself two direct evidences of authorship appear.
In 1:1 the author claims that his present work is the continuation of another volume. The "former treatise" *(ton prōton logon)*
to Theophilus is unquestionably the Gospel of Luke. Not only
is this conclusion strongly attested by early Christian writings,
but the similarity of literary style, vocabulary, and addressee
makes this obvious. The beginning of Acts dovetails neatly with
the ending of Luke's Gospel, indicating that the author was
resuming the same narrative with just a brief recapitulation
and then carrying it forward.

A second clue to the author is found in the use of the first
person "we" at certain places in the narrative. Inasmuch as the
style is the same throughout the book, the evidence argues for

only one author. The most obvious explanation of the "we" sections is that on those occasions the author was personally present. The "we" sections occur in three places:

16:10-17   Troas to Philippi (second missionary journey)
20:6–21:18   Philippi to Jerusalem (third missionary journey)
27:1–28:16   Voyage to Rome

All these sections record travels of Paul. Hence the author must be found among Paul's companions. R. B. Rackham has tabulated from Paul's writings and from Acts the names of Paul's associates during the "we" sections.[1] From this tabulation he is able to eliminate all but two — Titus and Luke. Because of the preference given to Luke by the early church, and the similarity to the Gospel of Luke, the credit for authorship most certainly belongs to the gentile Luke, the "beloved physician" (Col. 4:14) and companion of Paul from the second journey until the end of his life (II Tim. 4:11).

Date

Events in Acts carry the reader to the second year of Paul's residence in Rome (28:30). This was A.D. 61 or 62, and would seem to mark the earliest possible date for the writing of the book. Evidence pinpointing the time of writing subsequent to A.D. 62 is largely inferential, and two opinions are commonly espoused by those who hold to Lukan authorship.[2]

The first view dates the book between A.D. 62 and 64. The following are the chief reasons for this dating. (1) The outcome of Paul's Roman imprisonment would surely have been mentioned if the author had known it. The prominence of Paul in the latter half of Acts makes it most unlikely that his release or his death would have gone unnoticed if either had occurred. (2) No reference is made to the fall of Jerusalem, a city receiving much attention in Acts. The cataclysmic nature of this event in A.D. 70 and its implications for the Christian movement would hardly have been overlooked by the first-rate historian that Luke was. (3) No mention appears of Nero's persecution of

---

[1]*The Acts of the Apostles,* 14th ed. (London, 1951), p. xvi.
[2]For a concise but excellent discussion, see Donald Guthrie, *New Testament Introduction: The Gospels and Acts* (Chicago, 1965), pp. 397-315.

Christians after the fire of Rome in A.D. 64. Luke has concentrated on bringing his narrative to its culmination at Rome,
and the first imperial persecution was certainly of historical
significance.

The other view puts the writing between A.D. 70 and 85. It
is largely based upon the consideration that Acts was subsequent
to Luke's Gospel, a document that was written in the 60's.
Furthermore, it is sometimes suggested that Luke's Gospel
has altered the prophecy of the destruction of Jerusalem (in the
Olivet Discourse) to make it conform to the fact, thus demand-
ing a date subsequent to A.D. 70. Conservative scholars would
reject this reason, although some still hold to this later dating.
Luke's death sometime around A.D. 85 would mark the latest
possible date for Acts.

Purpose

Acts is addressed to Theophilus (1:1, 2), the same person
named "most excellent Theophilus" in the address of the third
Gospel. There is no warrant for allegorizing the name to refer
to all believers (i.e., each Christian being a "lover of God"),
especially in view of Luke 1:3 which employs the title "most
excellent" (kratiste), used every other time in the NT of individuals (Acts 23:26; 24:3; 26:25). Although it is likely that Luke
had a wider audience in view than just one man, the address
to Theophilus should not be understood as a mere dedication.
This volume, as well as the Gospel, was actually written to him.
Perhaps he was a wealthy and influential convert who helped
with the expense of publication. The Gospel had told the story
of Jesus' life, or as Luke put it, "all that Jesus began both to do
and to teach," up until the ascension. The implication is that
Jesus was continuing to work, only now it was through Spirit-
filled apostles. This second volume to Theophilus would recount this new phase of the Christian movement. Sir William
Ramsay thought that Luke had planned a third volume, but
was apparently prevented from writing it.[3] He based his idea
on the reference to the Gospel of Luke as the "first" (prōton)

---

[3]St. Paul the Traveller and the Roman Citizen (Grand Rapids, reprinted.,
1949), p. 23.

volume, rather than the "former" (*proteron*) in Acts 1:1. However, this distinction cannot be rigidly pressed, for *protōs* is used numerous times in the NT to denote the first of two (Matt. 21:28; I Cor. 14:30; Heb. 8:7, 9:15). Whatever Luke's plans may have been, only the two volume work Luke-Acts was ever known to the early church.

As Luke pursued his thesis, he developed it by showing how Christ instructed his followers to stay in Jerusalem until the Holy Spirit would empower them for their task of being witnesses. Once that had happened, he then traced the expansion of the movement throughout Judea and the rest of Palestine until it reached the heart of the empire — Rome itself. He did not endeavor to recount all the acts of all the apostles. As a good historian he has selected those incidents which were crucial to the movement, and from them he has written this thrilling record.

One further purpose seems to have been in the author's mind. There is an unmistakable apologetic emphasis as Luke sets forth time after time how Christianity is not a subversive movement. On various occasions the Christian enterprise comes into confrontation with Roman officials, and each time it is made clear that nothing treasonable is involved. These occasions were at Cyprus (13:7-12), Philippi (16:19-39), Thessalonica (17:6-9), Athens (17:18-34), Corinth (18:12-17), Ephesus (19:31-41), and at Caesarea before Felix (24:23-27), Festus (25:14-21, 25), and Agrippa (26:30-32). Although it can hardly be maintained that Acts was written expressly as defense material for Paul's trial (absence of any mention of the trial argues against it, as well as its being addressed to Theophilus), the clear depiction of the Christian movement as legally respectable served a good purpose in its own right. Any serious investigator of Christianity would surely have been interested in these matters, especially when Christians were often maligned and frequently persecuted as enemies of the state. The Book of Acts served to set forth the Christian faith in its true perspective as that which Christ had instituted, and which by his Spirit dwelling in men he was spreading throughout the world.

THE BEGINNING: JERUSALEM
Acts 1—7

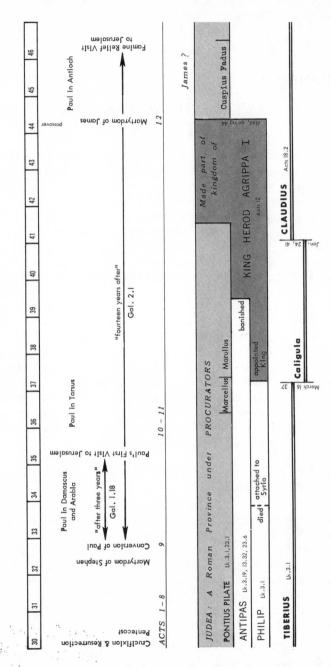

APOSTOLIC MINISTRY

| 30 | 31 | 32 | 33 | 34 | 35 | 36 | 37 | 38 | 39 | 40 | 41 | 42 | 43 | 44 | 45 | 46 |

Crucifixion & Resurrection
Pentecost

Martyrdom of Stephen

Paul in Damascus and Arabia

Conversion of Paul

"after three years"
Gal. 1.18

Paul's First Visit to Jerusalem

Paul in Tarsus

"fourteen years after"
Gal. 2.1

Martyrdom of James

Paul in Antioch

Passover

Famine Relief Visit to Jerusalem

James ?

ACTS 1 – 8   9   10 – 11   12

JUDEA: A Roman Province under PROCURATORS   Lk.3.1, 13.32, 23.6

PONTIUS PILATE   Lk.3.1, 23.1   Marcellus | Marullus

Made part of kingdom of

KING HEROD AGRIPPA I   Acts 12

Cuspius Fadus

ANTIPAS   Lk.3.19, 13.32, 13.6   died

banished

appointed King

died, spring 44

PHILIP   Lk.3.1   attached to Syria

TIBERIUS   Lk.3.1   Caligula   March 16   37   Jan. 24, 41   CLAUDIUS   Acts 18.2

Fig. 1. Time Chart I: A.D. 30-46

Chapter 1

THE CHURCH IS BORN
(Acts 1, 2)

Luke's first volume (the Gospel according to Luke) had already been written and sent to Theophilus. In it the dramatic account was given of the life and ministry of Jesus Christ. Luke had traced the beginnings of the Christian movement even prior to Jesus, for he began with the annunciation of the birth of John the Baptist. His narrative related the nativity of Christ, gave a brief glimpse of his childhood, and then concentrated upon the remarkable deeds and teachings of his public ministry. His Gospel concluded with a vivid description of the crucifixion and resurrection, and a very brief statement of the ascension. In Acts 1:1, however, this entire account is summarized as what "Jesus began both to do and to teach." The implication is that what follows in this second volume known to us as Acts describes what Jesus Christ *continues* to do since his ascension as the Holy Spirit empowered believers to carry on the purposes of Christ. Thus we find the apostles performing miracles but attributing the cause to Jesus Christ (Acts 3:6, 4:10, 9:34). Christ is presented as acting directly in the case of Stephen (7:55) and Paul (9:5). For further discussion of verses 1-2, the reader is referred to the Introduction.

I. THE FINAL INSTRUCTION OF THE DISCIPLES (1:3-8)

A. *Presentation of Many Proofs* (1:3)

Following Christ's resurrection and prior to the ascension, he made numerous bodily appearances to believers which are recorded in the Gospels. On these occasions he talked with them (Luke 24:13-32), ate with them (Luke 24:41-43), and showed them his scars (Luke 24:13-32), thus demonstrating irrefutably the reality of his physical resurrection. His "speaking of the things pertaining to the kingdom of God" was also a proof that the risen Christ was the same person who had been

21

crucified, for he continued his same teaching. The content of this post-resurrection teaching on the kingdom is not recorded here, but it is reflected in the teaching of the apostles later in Acts and in the Epistles. Such matters as the harmonization of a suffering Messiah with a true and glorious kingdom must have been included. No doubt the Messianic significance of many OT passages was also explained (for example, Acts 1:16, 20; 2:16-36; 3:18-26).

B. *Promise of the Spirit* (1:4, 5)

On one of the occasions when Christ was assembled together[1] with them, he reminded the disciples of the coming of the Holy Spirit. He had explained to them in the upper room discourse on the evening before the crucifixion that he and the Father would send the Holy Spirit to take the place of the absent Jesus (John 14-16, particularly 14:16, 26; 15:26; 16:7). Now he tells them to wait in Jerusalem for this promise to be fulfilled (it actually occurred about ten days later). Just as John had baptized with water as his instrument, so they would be baptized with[2] the Holy Spirit. This act would create out of these individual believers a spiritual union called by Paul "one body" — the body of Christ. "For by one Spirit are we all baptized into one body" (I Cor. 12:13).

C. *Problem of the Kingdom* (1:6-8)

Although Jesus had been teaching the disciples about his kingdom, not only throughout his ministry (Matt. 4:17) but also during his post-resurrection appearances (Acts 1:3), one feature about the kingdom still puzzled them: "Wilt thou at this time restore the kingdom to Israel?" It is obvious from their question that the kingdom referred to was the one which the Jews looked for Messiah to establish (Isa. 9:6-7; 11:10-12). Many conclude that this question indicated a complete mis-

---

[1]The verb translated in KJV and ASV as "assembled together"(*sunalizomenos*) occurs only here in the NT. It is possible that it is derived from *halas* ("salt"), and should be translated as "eating salt with" or more generally "eating with" (so ASV margin).

[2]The preposition "with" is the Greek *en*, the same one translated "by" in I Cor. 12:13, and denotes instrument in both places.

understanding of the nature of Christ's kingdom, reflecting a preoccupation with mere temporal rule. However, it must be noted that Christ's answer did not say that there would be no literal kingdom. He merely said that the time of establishment would not now be revealed to them.

The reason why the disciples must not concern themselves with pinpointing the inaugurating of Israel's restored kingdom was that they had a new task to perform. They were to be Christ's witnesses after the empowering of the Holy Spirit had occurred. They were to testify to the person of Christ, his teachings, his sacrificial death and his resurrection. The twelve (actually only eleven at this moment) were witnesses of Christ as no others could be for they had been with him from the beginning (John 15:26, 27), and Christ promised that the Spirit would cause them to remember what they had heard from his lips (John 14:26; 16:13-15). In addition to their initial preaching, their production of the NT stands as the primary testimony, and all who subsequently have "witnessed" for Christ base their testimony upon the authority of those first witnesses (i.e., the NT). Historically the disciples performed their witness first in Jerusalem. From there the message was extended throughout the rest of Palestine. With the journeys of Paul, the gospel of Christ was carried to the heart of the Roman Empire — to Rome itself. A look at the outline will show that Luke has constructed the Book of Acts upon this historical sequence.

II. THE ASCENSION OF CHRIST (1:9-11)

Throughout the period of the post-resurrection forty days, Jesus had frequently appeared to the disciples, and during the intervals he had disappeared. Each time, apparently, they had no reason to suppose that he would not reappear shortly, and until this time he had not disappointed them. Now there was a difference. Jesus had led the little group to the Mount of Olives, east of Jerusalem across the Kidron Valley and near the village of Bethany (Luke 24:50). The mention of the distance as "a Sabbath day's journey" did not necessarily mean that the event occurred on a Sabbath. Rather it was a common expres-

Fig. 2. The Mount of Olives on the horizon east of the Old City of Jerusalem. The traditional site of the Ascension is marked by the smaller of the two towers on the skyline. Levant Photo Service

sion of measurement, based upon the rabbinical regulation as to the distance a Jew was allowed to travel without violating Exodus 16:29.[3] From this impressive height overlooking Jerusalem, Jesus ascended to heaven. He did not suddenly vanish as before (Luke 24:31), but "while they were looking" *(blepontōn auton)* he was taken up. Apparently it was a gradual removal until a cloud enveloped him and hid him from their view. This cloud was probably the Shekinah, the divine cloud of glory which rested above the tabernacle in the days of Moses, signifying the presence of the Lord (Exod. 40:34).

As the disciples beheld this awesome scene, two men in white garments appeared. These two have been identified as Enoch and Elijah (the two OT saints who left this earth without dying), or Moses and Elijah (the two who appeared with Jesus at the transfiguration, who are also sometimes identified with the two witnesses of Revelation 11:3-6). They are more commonly understood as angels. Luke has previously described angels as "men" in Luke 24:4, and dazzling white garments are a frequent apparel in angelic appearances (Mark 16:5; Luke 24:4).

The apostles were addressed as "Galileans" (Judas, apparently the only Judean [from Kerioth] was now gone). This designation is employed of them again in Acts 2:7. Through the message of the two in white, they were informed that Christ would return, although the different circumstances of his leaving this time indicated that this was not just another momentary departure. Christ's promised return would be "in the same manner" as they had seen him depart. Many of the features which characterized his departure are mentioned elsewhere in Scripture in connection with the second coming. Some dispensationalists explain this as a reference to the rapture of the church, preceding the actual return of Christ to earth by seven years. However, it seems better to interpret it as Christ's glorious return to usher in the age to come. At that time the Bible says he will

---

[3] The Sabbath day's journey was computed as 2,000 cubits (approximately 3,000 feet). This distance to the Mount of Olives agrees with Josephus who says it is five stadia (3,000 feet) from Jerusalem. *Antiquities of the Jews,* XX 8:6.

come with clouds of glory (Dan. 7:13; Matt. 24:30; Rev. 1:7), and will stand upon the Mount of Olives (Zech. 14:4).

III. THE CHOICE OF MATTHIAS (1:12-26)

A. *The Prayer* (1:12-14)

The apostles returned to Jerusalem from the Mount of Olives, and entered "the upper room." The use of the definite article in the Greek text points to a particular upper room, perhaps the same one where the last supper with Jesus had occurred. In any case it was the headquarters of the believers in Jerusalem, for the imperfect tense form "they were abiding" denotes their habitual activity. In all likelihood the place was part of a large home. Efforts to identify it as the home of John Mark's mother (as in Acts 12:12) are interesting but not conclusive. Nor is it likely that this upper room was in the temple (Luke 24:53). It is best to understand that the disciples divided their time between the temple (at regular worship hours) and the upper room.

The group present in this upper room was composed of the eleven, the women (apparently the ones who had followed Jesus from Galilee, Luke 8:2, 3; Mark 15: 40, 41), Mary the mother of Jesus (this is her last recorded appearance in the NT), Jesus' half-brothers (who had been unbelievers until very recently, John 7:3-5), and others to bring the total to 120. This was not the total number of believers, although it may have been all who were in Jerusalem, for Jesus had appeared to over five hundred at one time after his resurrection.[4] How interesting that among those waiting for the promise of the Spirit was Mary, who apparently had the same need as the others. The chief activity of the group during this time was prayer,[5] although the following verses indicate that matters of business also were conducted.

---

[4] I Corinthians 15:6, referring to an event in Galilee probably.

[5] It should not be inferred that they were necessarily praying for the Spirit, for the Holy Spirit came in answer to Christ's promise, and the disciples were told only to wait for its fulfilment (Acts 1:4).

B. *The Problem* (1:15-22)

During the days of waiting Peter acted as spokesman for the group and defined a problem that many of them must have pondered. How could an apostle whom Jesus himself selected have become a traitor? Jesus had already related Judas to Psalm 41:9 (John 13:18, 19). The OT passage referred historically to Ahithophel's defection to David's enemies. Since David himself was God's appointed king, many times Scripture treats him as typical of Christ, the unique Anointed One, and David's enemy becomes a type of Jesus' enemy. The risen Christ had opened the understanding of many such Scriptures to his disciples (Luke 24:44-46). By relating the act of Judas to prophecy, Peter showed that it was no embarrassment to God's program, even though it was a heinous deed.

The field which Judas obtained with the blood money was actually purchased by the priests (Matt. 27:6-8). They probably purchased it in Judas' name since it was legally his money. Although it is often asserted that Acts and Matthew are based upon two differing traditions, the two Biblical accounts are not irreconcilable. Judas could have hanged himself (Matthew), and later when his corpse was cut down, it could have broken with the gruesome results mentioned here (note the similar result when people were thrown down from a high rock, II Chron. 25:12). Whether the name "field of blood" is derived from its purchase with "blood money" (Matt. 27:6-8), or because Judas' demise actually occurred on the premises is a question which cannot be settled with certainty at present.

Two OT passages were quoted by Peter to show that the apostasy of Judas demanded his replacement. Psalm 69:25 spoke of the removal of the psalmist's enemy, and Psalm 109:8 mentions the replacement of an enemy by someone else. Peter, enlightened no doubt by Christ's own teaching in recent days (Luke 24:44-46; Acts 1:3), regarded these references as typical of Judas, the traitor to God's Anointed One. It should be noted that it was the defection of Judas, not his death, that caused the replacement. No effort was made to replace James when he died by martyrdom (Acts 12:2).

Two requirements were necessary for one to fill the vacancy

left by Judas. (1) He must have been a follower of Christ throughout his ministry, not therefore a recent convert (note the description by Jesus in John 15:27). (2) He must be a witness of the resurrection, as were the eleven.

C. The Solution (1:23-26)

Two men were put forward who fit these requirements. Neither man was mentioned in the Gospels. If the group felt qualified to narrow the choice to two, why not the final one? In all probability, therefore, they were the only ones who qualified, and thus the congregation did not really do any choosing at all. Prayer followed, not to direct God's choice, but to ascertain his will. The group believed that God had already chosen, and merely needed to indicate that choice to them.

The casting of lots followed the prayer. This was an OT procedure, and was done that God might indicate his will. "The lot is cast into the lap, but the whole disposing thereof is of the Lord" (Prov. 16:33). This was the method prescribed by God for choosing the scapegoat in the Day of Atonement ritual (Lev. 16:8). It was not a vote. Usually stones were used, either a white and a black one, or stones on which the names of the candidates were written. There is no further evidence of this practice among Christians after this instance. The casting of the lots resulted in the choice of Matthias as the twelfth apostle, and thus the apostolic body was complete by the time of Pentecost.

Some have felt that Peter and the others acted in haste and in error.[6] They have argued that God intended for Paul to be the twelfth apostle. The use of the lot is alleged to show a lack of reliance upon the Holy Spirit. Most students, however, see no such problem, and base their conclusion on the following: (1) Scripture nowhere suggests that the choice of Matthias was wrong. The action of the disciples was based on the OT, they prayed for God's will to be done, and they used a legitimate method of ascertaining God's will in that period before Pente-

---

[6]So G. Campbell Morgan, The Acts of the Apostles (New York: 1924), p. 24; E. M. Blaiklock, The Acts of the Apostles, in The Tyndale New Testament Commentaries (Grand Rapids: 1959), p. 53.

cost. (2) If the choice of Matthias was wrong, then Peter was guilty of misusing OT prophecy. (3) The fact that Paul is called an apostle is no argument against Matthias, for others in the NT are called apostles (e.g., Acts 14:4, 14). Hence Paul can be called an apostle without conflicting with the twelve. (4) Paul had a unique ministry separate from the twelve. He clearly distinguished himself from them, and never argued that he should be included in that particular group (I Cor. 15:5, 8).

IV. THE COMING OF THE SPIRIT (2:1-13)

A. *The Arrival* (2:1-3)

At last the feast day of Pentecost arrived. This feast (the name "Pentecost" means "fiftieth") occurred annually fifty days after the presenting of the first sheaf of the harvest on the day following the Passover sabbath (Lev. 23:15, 16), and commemorated the harvest. The disciples were still together, whether in the same upper room as before or in the temple ("house" in vs. 2 could apply to either). As the promised baptism of the Holy Spirit occurred, two physical evidences appeared. A sound like a mighty wind filled the house, enveloping the group and suggesting perhaps the corporate nature of what had transpired. The second evidence was the appearance of fire-like tongues distributing themselves[7] upon each one present. This provided visible evidence that each person was a participant in this baptism of the Spirit. That this was the fulfilment of Jesus' promise is clearly stated in Acts 11:15-17 (cf. 1:4, 5). Baptism by the Spirit made them into one spiritual body, the body of Christ (I Cor. 12:13).

B. *The Results* (2:4-6)

Following this baptism of the Spirit, the believers were all filled with the Spirit." This too was accompanied by outward evidence — speaking with "other tongues." Filling with the Spirit is mentioned in the NT as a recurring experience for Christians. Some of these same persons who were filled with

---

[7]The participle *diamerizomenai* is a present, and probably is middle voice, yielding the sense "dividing themselves," rather than "cloven" (KJV).

the Spirit on Pentecost were filled again in 4:8 and 4:31. It has to do with the control of the believer by the Spirit so that he may serve God in some effective way. Spirit *baptism*, however, differs from Spirit *filling*, and is never mentioned in Scripture as occurring to the same persons more than once, for it is that spiritual work of God whereby one is made part of the body of Christ (I Cor. 12:13), an act needing no repetition.

The tongues spoken by the believers at Pentecost resulted in the hearing by people of many nationalities of utterances in their own dialects. The speakers used languages not hitherto known by them but perfectly understood by the hearers. At other key points in revelatory history, supernatural phenomena had occurred, so that these amazing events are not surprising at this momentous time (note the miraculous happenings at the giving of the Law, Exod. 19:16, 18).

When the sound of their voices[8] was heard, a crowd quickly gathered. Perhaps the speakers came out into the streets, so that in a very short time thousands of Jewish residents[9] of Jerusalem became witnesses of the event.

C. *The Reaction* (2:7-13)

Amazement seized the hearers, although some of them explained the speaking in tongues as drunkenness.[10] Paul also used the illustration of alcoholic intoxication as a contrast to Spirit filling (Eph. 5:18). The similarity lies in the control of the person by another force, either a physical intoxicant or the Holy Spirit.

The tongues of Pentecost have been explained in various ways

---

[8]*Phōnēs* never means "report," and thus "noised abroad" (KJV) is not correct. Although the term in vs. 6 might refer to the noise of the mighty wind, it is not the same word as used for "sound" in vs. 2 (*ēchos*). Most likely it refers to the sound of the tongues speakers.

[9]"Dwelling" (*katoikountes*) normally denotes a more permanent residing than simply a temporary visit to the feast. Perhaps this describes Jews who had returned to their ancestral homeland to end their days.

[10]The word for "new wine" is *gleukous*, but it cannot mean freshly made wine since it was too early in the spring for the current vintage. References to ancient methods for keeping wine sweet all year can be found, but the usage here is clearly to wine that could intoxicate. The same word is used in the LXX of Job 32:19, where it also must mean fermenting wine.

from that day to this. Conservative scholars have usually adopted one of the following views. (1) These tongues are thought to be the same as those employed at Corinth, and both consisted of ecstatic speech. The only difference lay in the means of interpretation. At Pentecost the ecstatic speaking was miraculously interpreted in the ears of those present. At Corinth a human interpreter was required (I Cor. 14:27, 28). This explanation is certainly possible, although it requires two miracles instead of one. Furthermore, Acts 2:4 says they began to "speak with other tongues," and verse 6 (and 8) says each foreigner heard them "speaking in his own language." Also if the hearing was a miracle, why would some charge the disciples with drunkenness? Was the miracle imperfect?[11] (2) These tongues were the same as those at Corinth, and both were foreign languages. This view has the advantage of requiring only one explanation for all the Biblical phenomena, and since foreign languages were almost certainly involved at Pentecost, this explanation is extended to Corinth as well. It should not be overlooked, however, that there were differences. One type required a human interpreter; the other did not. One type was intended to bring a message to outsiders; the other was primarily for private edification (I Cor. 14:2, 4, 19). We cannot conclude that tongues were foreign languages employed for missionary work because Paul apparently never evangelized with tongues although possessing the Corinthian-type gift (I Cor. 14:18, 19).

(3) This view holds that the tongues of Pentecost differed from those at Corinth. Those at Pentecost were a temporary speaking in foreign languages, but those at Corinth were ecstatic speech. The differences in their respective Biblical descriptions are held to be sufficient justification for recognizing that glossolalia may take different forms, and that the situation at

[11]A variation of this view has been advocated recently by C. R. Smith. Biblical glossolalia is described as a non-miraculous expression of devotion resulting from the Holy Spirit's work in the believer. At Pentecost the ecstatic speech must have included some sub-consciously remembered foreign words and phrases as directed by the Spirit which the hearers recognized. Charles R. Smith, *Biblical Conclusions Concerning Tongues.* Unpublished doctoral dissertation, Grace Theological Seminary, 1970.

Pentecost was unique. That the supernatural phenomena at
Pentecost (including also the mighty wind and the fire-like
tongues) were not repeated is no more surprising than the non-
repetition of the physical manifestations at Sinai when the Law
was given.

V. THE PREACHING OF PETER (2:14-40)

A. *Introduction* (2:14-21)

Peter acted as spokesman for the believers and explained the
miraculous happenings. These events were not the results of
wine (it was only 9:00 a.m.,[12] an hour when even drunkards
were not yet intoxicated), but were related to the prophecy of
Joel 2:28-32. For Peter, this outpouring of the Spirit began
the period known in Scripture as the "last days" or the "last
hour" (I John 2:18), and thus the whole Christian era is included in the expression. This introduction would arrest the
attention of any Jew.

B. *Argument* (2:22-36)

The proposition which Peter argues is that Jesus is the
Messiah (Christ) and Lord (vs. 36). Three proofs are given
to the vast audience which had gathered.

1. The works of Jesus on earth substantiated this fact (vs. 22).
By miracles (*dunamesi*, deeds of great power viewed here as
supernatural), and wonders (*terasi*, acts which produced wonderment and awe among the beholders) and signs (*sēmeiois*,
deeds and words which served as credentials or proofs of his
person and mission), Jesus had shown that he was sent of God.
These were well known, having occurred frequently during his
public ministry.

2. The resurrection of Jesus substantiated this fact (vss.
23-32). Peter was well aware that most of his audience, though
willing perhaps to admit the miraculous deeds of Jesus, would
reject his messiahship because he had been executed as a

---

[12]By Jewish reckoning the new day began at sundown and consisted of
twelve hours of darkness followed by twelve hours of daylight. The third
hour of the day was thus about 9 o'clock in the morning.

criminal. Therefore, he showed from Psalm 16:8-11 that Messiah's death was included in the will of God and was predicted in Scripture (even though men who killed him were not excused from guilt for they were called "wicked"). When David wrote, "Thou wilt not leave my soul in sheol, neither wilt thou suffer thine Holy One to see corruption," he could not have meant himself, for his body did return to the dust of the tomb. As a prophet, he was speaking of his great messianic Heir, and of the fact that the death of Christ would not result in abandonment to sheol nor disintegration of his body, but that death would be followed by resurrection. Since the resurrection of Christ was predicted in the OT, obviously his death must also have been foreseen. Peter and the other apostles were now testifying that the resurrection of Christ had indeed occurred, in perfect fulfilment of David's prophecy.

3. The outpouring of the Spirit by Jesus also demonstrated the truth of Peter's argument (vss. 33-36). Not only was Jesus a man whom God had approved by granting the power to do great works, and by raising him from the dead, but the ascension and outpouring of the Spirit demonstrated the Lordship of Christ on a plane far higher than the earthly. Peter interprets Psalm 110:1 of Christ (just as Jesus himself had done in Matt. 22:41-45). The psalm depicts Messiah (David's "Lord") as seated at God's right hand, the position of honor and authority. The apostles had watched him ascend to heaven, and the sending of the Spirit just as Jesus had promised proved that he was in the exalted position necessary to perform such a feat.

C. *Application* (2:37-40)

The inquiry of the hearers brought the instruction from Peter that they should repent and be baptized in the name of Jesus Christ. Then they too would receive the Holy Spirit, just as the original group. "Repent" *(metanoēsate)* means to change the mind and here includes all aspects of conversion including faith. It is coupled with baptism, the outward public confession that this repentance has occurred. It is incorrect to link "for the remission of sins" solely with the baptism so as to suggest that water baptism brings forgiveness of sin. A similar statement by

Peter in Acts 3:19 shows that what brings remission of sins is not water baptism but repentance and conversion. The close connection of baptism with repentance should not surprise us, however, for the NT always assumes that a true Christian will obey his Lord and be baptized. It may be helpful to translate "for the remission" (eis aphesin) as "with reference to the remission," and avoid erroneous notions.[13]

VI. THE DESCRIPTION OF THE CHURCH (2:41-47)

A. Membership (2:41)

Three thousand heeded the admonition of Peter and received Christian baptism in water. These were added[14] to the original group from the upper room. The little band of believers now had sufficient visibility in the city that their presence could not be ignored.

B. General Activity (2:42-45)

The Christian group, the vast majority of whom were new converts, spent their time in direct spiritual activity. They received instruction from the apostles, the qualified witnesses of Christ and the resurrection (Matt. 28:19). Later their testimony was written and became our NT. Christian fellowship with one another was also a characteristic of these first believers, made possible through their common sharing of the life of Christ. Fellowship both with Christ and with other Christians is a basic ingredient of Christianity. The presence of the articles in the expression "the breaking of the bread"[15] indicates more than just eating. It appears to be a reference to the symbolic eating of the Bread and Cup, partaken in connection with a sacred meal, the Agape. Both I Corinthians 11 and patristic literature reveal that the Eucharist was preceded by a religious

---

[13]This use of eis is found in such references as Luke 14:35; Matt. 3:11 and 12:41.

[14]This whole paragraph (vss. 41-47) emphasizes the visible relationships of the believers. Hence "were added" (prosetethēsan) should be understood of their addition to the group of Christians, not of their mystical addition "to the Lord."

[15]Greek: tēi klasei tou artou.

meal.[16] The offering of prayers also characterized the general activity of the church.

The apostles, in addition to their teaching ministry, performed wonders and signs in the city. One of them is recorded in Chapter 3. The believers themselves shared in a community of goods. This was not compulsory as Acts 5:4 proves. It arose out of brotherly love in a situation where actual physical need was occurring. It was a local situation at Jerusalem, not enjoined on the whole church. However, the sending of alms to needy churches sprang from the same principle of spiritual brotherhood.

C. *Daily Life* (2:46, 47)

The Jerusalem Christians still worshipped daily at the temple and felt no inconsistency. Later the intense opposition of fanatical Jews made this more difficult, although Paul and other Jewish Christians still went to the temple at least at late as the 50's (Acts 22:26), and probably until its destruction in A.D. 70. No one house was large enough to accommodate the entire group, so they ate in various houses.[17] At this time the Christians had the respect of the whole city of Jerusalem. The reader will do well to pay close attention to this situation in Acts and notice the shift which eventually occurred. To all of this the Lord gave his blessing by adding daily "those being saved" *(tous sōzomenous).*

QUESTIONS FOR DISCUSSION

1. What prompted the disciples to ask Jesus about the restoration of Israel's kingdom?
2. How can the Acts description of the death of Judas and the field of blood be harmonized with the account in Matthew 27:3-10?
3. Were the apostles wrong in choosing the twelfth apostle?

---

[16]J. B. Lightfoot, *Apostolic Fathers* (London, 1889), Part II, Vol. II, p. 313, commenting on the Epistle of Ignatius *To the Smyrneans*. Also the *Didache* (see R. D. Hitchcock and Francis Brown, *Teaching of the Twelve Apostles* [New York, 1885], p. 19).

[17]"From house to house" is the KJV rendering of *kat' oikon,* which employs *kata* in the distributive sense and is better understood as "in various houses." The same use occurs in verse 47 in the phrase *kath' hēmeran,* "daily," or "on various days."

4. Do you think that the modern glossolalia is the same as the tongues of Pentecost?
5. What evidence is there in the Bible to help us decide whether such things as tongues speaking, wonders and signs, and the community of goods should be occurring today among Christians?
6. What is the difference between being baptized by the Spirit and being filled with the Spirit?

Chapter 2

A MIRACLE AND ITS AFTERMATH
(Acts 3:1—4:31)

During the early days of the new church, the apostles performed many miracles (2:43). Luke has picked out one of these for special mention, not because it was particularly spectacular (although it certainly was remarkable) but because it produced the first conflict between the church and outsiders. Until this time the church had been enjoying the favor of all the people (2:24). As a consequence of this miracle, however, the first opposition began.

I. THE HEALING OF THE LAME MAN (3:1-11)

Peter and John were entering the temple at the regular afternoon hour of prayer.[1] Twice daily the priest offered incense in the holy place of the temple, and devout Israelites would gather outside for prayers. (This was the task in which Zacharias was engaged when he was informed by an angel of the coming birth of John, Luke 1:8-22.) The early Christians continued synagogue attendance and temple worship, and saw no inconsistency. The impetus for their expulsion came later from enraged Jews, not from the Christian believers. Acts records this period of transition.

A lame man over forty years old (4:22) had been carried daily to the temple to ask alms from the worshippers. He had been a cripple since birth, and must have been a well-known sight among Jerusalem residents. Although there is disagreement over the precise identification of the "Beautiful Gate," it was most likely the eastern gate by which one entered the Women's Court from the Court of the Gentiles (or Outer Court).[2] The man was thus placed in an advantageous spot to

---

[1]The "ninth hour" Jewish time corresponds to 3 p.m. See note on 2:15.

[2]This gate is probably to be distinguished from the Nicanor Gate at the west end of the Women's Court. It is described by Josephus as made of Corinthian bronze and greatly excelled the others. It was 50 cubits high and

Fig. 3. Model of Herod's Temple. The Beautiful Gate may have been at the left center, leading from the Court of the Gentiles to the Court of the Women. Palphot Limited

accomplish his purpose. One may wonder idly why Jesus had never healed this man, since he had entered the temple on many occasions. However, Jesus did not heal every afflicted person in the nation (he healed only one at the pool of Bethesda, John 5). Perhaps the man was never able to get close to Jesus because of the throngs that were always crowding the temple, especially when Jesus was teaching there.

its doors were 40 cubits. "It was adorned after a most costly manner, as having much richer and thicker plates of silver and gold" (*Wars*, V.5) The text of Josephus is a bit confusing at this point, however, and some feel that the Corinthian Gate should be identified with the Nicanor Gate. Jack Finegan presents the possibility that the Beautiful Gate should be identified with the Shushan Gate (or Golden Gate) leading into the temple area, *The Archaeology of the NT* (Princeton, 1969), pp. 129, 130.

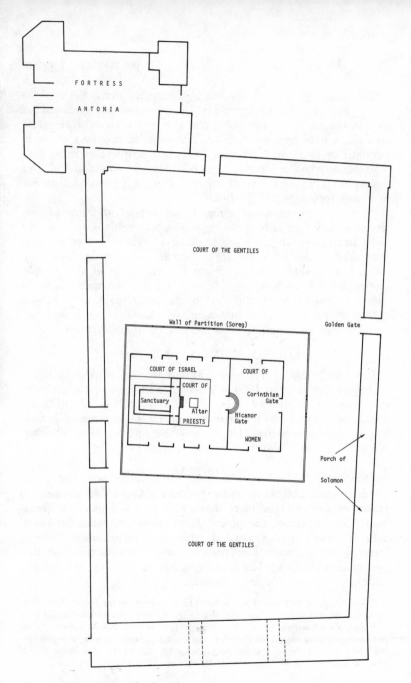

Fig. 4. Plan of Herod's Temple

The man did not ask for healing, only for alms. Peter, however, gave him something of far greater value. He commanded him in the name of Jesus Christ to rise and walk. The response was immediate and spectacular. The miracle supplied not only strength to joints and muscles, but also complete coordination. This man who had never learned to walk was suddenly an expert walking and leaping about. How appropriate that his first walk took him into the temple.

To the temple crowds the result was wonder and amazement. Because they had known the man and his problem, the miracle must have been all the more impressive. When the service was over, Peter and John left the sanctuary and made their way toward the colonnaded porch on the east side of the temple mount, known as Solomon's Porch.[3] The healed man clung to them, no doubt continuing his joyous outcries. A huge crowd gathered quickly, aware that a miracle had occurred, and desiring either explanation or further miraculous displays.

II. PETER'S SECOND SERMON (3:12-26)

Peter took the opportunity afforded by the miracle to make sure that the people did not miss its significance. He stressed the source of the miraculous power, and related it to God's Messianic plans for Israel. It was a message which every Jewish hearer should have found extremely impressive. The following propositions were asserted by the sermon.

A. *Jesus Had Healed the Man* (3:12-16)

The miracle had not been the product of the apostles' inherent power or unusual godliness. Rather, it was the name of Jesus which had furnished the power. Peter does not mean that some magical power was associated with the proper name "Jesus." "Name" often stands for "person," and includes all that the person is and does.[4] Thus "faith in his name" (vs. 16) means faith in Christ and his power to heal.

---

[3]This porch is mentioned again in 5:12 as a sort of unofficial gathering place for the Christians. Jesus had also taught at this spot (John 10:23).

[4]Peter may have reflected the common Jewish practice of avoiding the unnecessary use of words for God, lest one use God's name in vain. Frequently the Hebrew *šēm* (name) stood in place of the designation of deity (e.g., Lev. 24:11).

Jesus is referred to by a number of Messianic titles in this sermon. The God of Abraham, Isaac, and Jacob is described as glorifying his "servant"[5] Jesus. This is the same designation for Messiah as used in Isaiah 42:1-9 and 52:13–53:12 (LXX). The "Holy One of Israel" was a well-known name for Messiah (Ps. 16:10; Isa. 31:1; Mark 1:24; I John 2:20), and "the Righteous one" was likewise often used (Isa. 53:11; Zech. 9:9; I John 2:1). To call Christ the "Prince of life"[6] was to designate him as the one whose victory over death has made him the forerunner or leader of others. His resurrection qualified him for this title, and he is now the "Prince" who provides salvation and assurance of resurrection life (the same title is employed in Heb. 2:10 and 12:2).

In spite of Christ's clear Messianic credentials, the nation had rejected him, overriding Pilate's stated intention of releasing him. They preferred the murderer Barabbas (Luke 23:18, 19), and had paradoxically killed the Prince of life! God, however, had raised him from the dead, and Peter and John, as well as others bore unshakable testimony to the fact for they had seen him since his resurrection. It was this Jesus, indicated by the titles used of him by Peter to be the promised Messiah, who had miraculously healed the man standing before them.

B. *The Suffering of Jesus Fulfilled His Messiahship* (3:17, 18)

Doubtless many in Peter's Jewish audience would have been agreeable to much of the preceding statement. They would not have been averse to accepting the idea of a genuine miracle, nor were they unfamiliar with Jesus' reputation as a miracle worker. The problem they faced was identifying Jesus as their conquering Messiah in the light of the crucifixion. The offense of the cross was the great obstacle to Jewish acceptance of Jesus as the Christ. Peter sought to answer this problem in the second part of his message by showing that Messiah's suffering had been prophesied by the OT prophets. Thus the crucifixion was not a disaster to God's program. It did not disqualify Jesus from the Messianic office. OT Scripture had foreseen the suffering of Messiah in such passages as Isaiah 53.

---

[5]Greek: *paida.*
[6]Greek: *ton archēgon tēs zōēs.*

Although Peter had accused his audience of guilt in delivering up Jesus and denying him (vs. 13), he nevertheless attributed it to their ignorance. This, of course, was quite true, although it was an inexcusable ignorance. They possessed the Scripture, and had abundant reason to recognize the Messiahship of Jesus. Of particular interest is Peter's reference to "your rulers." Does this imply that already the infant church considered itself as distinct to some extent from the Jewish nation, even though the Christians still attended Jewish worship? Whatever the underlying reason, Peter places the blame on the people and their leaders who had used their authority to stir up the populace against Jesus. Yet he also says it was ignorance on their part. By this softened approach, he hoped to gain from his hearers a reversal of their attitude.

C. *The Delay in Establishing the Messianic Blessings Was Due to Jewish Unbelief* (3:19-26)

A Jew who listened carefully to Peter's argument might have still one more problem. If Jesus had healed the lame man by supernatural power as an evidence of his Messiahship, and if it would be admitted that the OT did, in fact, predict a suffering Messiah, there was still the problem of the Messianic blessings which he was supposed to bring. If Jesus really was the Messiah, where was the Messianic kingdom? Peter's answer was that his hearers must repent in order that their sins might be blotted out. Only then would Jesus Christ return from heaven to bring "seasons of refreshing" and "times of restoration"[7] in accord with OT prophecy. These two expressions appear to be similar with perhaps a slightly different emphasis, the former describing the results of Christ's return and the latter naming the time and the method.

Moses had spoken of Messianic times when he mentioned the coming of a "prophet like unto me" (Deut. 18:15). Both Peter and Stephen interpreted that prophecy of Christ (Acts 7:37). The reference to Samuel as giving Messianic prophecy is more difficult. Bruce's explanation seems adequate: "Samuel was the

---

[7]"Restoration" (*apokatastaseōs*) is a cognate of the verb used by the disciples in 1:6 when they asked about the restoration of Israel's kingdom (*apokathistaneis*).

prophet who anointed David as king and spoke of the establishment of his kingdom (I Sam. 13:14; 15:28; 16:13; 28:17), and
the promises made to David found their highest fulfillment in
Jesus."[8]

Inasmuch as Peter has harmonized the claim of Jesus with
OT prophecy, it was incumbent upon the hearers to respond in
faith to the message. As Jews it was their forefathers and particularly Abraham who had been the recipients of God's cov-
enant, and it was their prophets who had predicted Messiah's
coming. In their Scripture was the promise made to Abraham
that his seed would bring blessing to all the earth, and Peter
declares that Jesus, the descendant of Abraham, was the particular Seed in whom the promised blessing would come. It was
to the Jewish nation first of all, and specifically the generation
represented by these hearers at Solomon's Porch that God had
raised up[9] Jesus. They had the great privilege of responding to
the redemptive work of Christ and experiencing the spiritual
cleansing which is basic to the enjoyment of Messiah's kingdom.
The leaders of the nation had made their tragic decision some
weeks before. What would be the answer of those on Solomon's
Porch?

III. THE FIRST PERSECUTION (4:1-31)

A. *The Arrest* (4:1-4)

While the apostles (with Peter as spokesman) continued ad-
dressing the crowd, a group of temple officials came upon the
scene and took them into custody. These authorities were of
three classes. (1) The priests. The priesthood was divided into
twenty-four courses which served a week each in rotation. The
priests here must have been the members of the course that was
on duty in the temple that week. (2) The temple captain. This
officer (*stratēgos*), also referred to by Josephus under the same
title[10] (and called the Sagan in rabbinical literature), was the
head of the Levitical police force which maintained order in

---

[8]Bruce, *The Book of Acts*, p. 93.

[9]"Raised up" is probably to be understood in the sense of verse 22, rather
than of the resurrection.

[10]*War* II.17.2; VI.5.3; *Antiquities* XX.6.2; 9.3.

the temple. The Romans allowed the Jews to police the temple themselves. The captain ranked next to the high priest in authority within the temple precincts. (3) The Sadducees. These men, members of one of the religious parties of the Jews, had much influence in the temple because the high priest and his family belonged to the Sadducee party. This party was largely rationalistic, rejecting such supernatural concepts as angels and other spirit beings, and denied any literal resurrection (Acts 23:8). They were the first of the Jewish parties to persecute the church.

The reason Luke gives for the arrest was their teaching of the people and their proclamation of the resurrection. Here were two unknown persons who had gathered a tremendous crowd and were giving them instruction in the OT. They were men without any sort of credentials or official sanction. Although it does not seem that one needed to obtain permission to speak in the outer court of the temple (Jesus often did so, Luke 21:37), the presence of such a large crowd naturally produced some commotion, and the officials were irritated at this unannounced, and in their view, presumptuous meeting. A deeper reason lay in the content of Peter's preaching. As he[11] spoke of the resurrection of Jesus (3:15, 21), this implied the validity of literal resurrection. If Jesus had truly risen from the dead, the foundation for denying the possibility of resurrection was destroyed. The resurrection of Christ was one of the basic themes of apostolic preaching, and is foundational to the Christian faith (I Cor. 15:12-19). It is not difficult to see why the first official opposition would come from the Sadducees.

The arrest was made in late afternoon (following the regular time of evening sacrifice and prayer held at 3 p.m. (Acts 3:1). Inasmuch as Jewish law forbade night trials (a law flagrantly violated in the case of Jesus), the two apostles were jailed overnight.

Even this serious turn of events did not choke off the progress of the gospel. New believers continued to be made, and the

---

[11]The use of the plural "they" in this context denotes that both Peter and John were understood as conducting this meeting. Even though Peter was the spokesman, it was obvious that John was associated with him and was equally responsible.

total number came to be *(egenēthē)* about 5000 men *(andrōn, males)*. This does not seem to count women and children. It is the last figure which Luke states, although he does give additional progress reports in general terms (Acts 5:14; 6:7; 9:31; 12:24; 16:5; 19:20; 28:31).

B. The Trial (4:5-22)

1. The Testimony (4:5-12)

The next morning the authorities gathered to take up the case of Peter and John. The reference to this group as "rulers and elders and scribes" identifies it as the Sanhedrin, the highest ruling body of the Jewish nation, composed of seventy members plus the high priest who served as president. The "rulers" are called elsewhere "chief priests" (Matt. 16:21), and were representatives of the twenty-four priestly courses. "Elders" were the tribal and family heads of the people. "Scribes" were the experts in interpreting the law. The Pharisean segment of the Sanhedrin was found among the scribes, although not all Pharisees were scribes. In the NT the Sanhedrin is variously referred to by naming all or some of its parts (note 4:23). On this occasion the Sanhedrin was heavily represented by Sadducean elements. Annas, a former high priest[12] who was still a powerful figure, and his son-in-law Caiaphas, who presently occupied the high priesthood, were both Sadducees, as well as others called here the "kindred of the high priest." John is called "Jonathan" in the Western text, and thus could be Jonathan the son of Annas who succeeded Caiaphas as high priest in A.D. 36.[13] Alexander is not otherwise known to us, but he and John were part of the high priestly group. The usual meeting place of the Sanhedrin was in the Chamber of Hewn Stone, probably situated west of the temple area.[14]

The Sanhedrin was acting within its jurisdiction when it convened to examine Peter and John. The Mosaic Law specified that whenever someone performed a miracle and used it as the

---

[12]Former high priests apparently still retained their title.
[13]Josephus *Antiquities* XVIII.4.3.
[14]Josephus *War* V.4.2. Certain identification is not possible at present, however. Some Talmudic sources place it within the temple precincts.

basis for teaching, he was to be examined, and if the teaching
were used to lead men away from the God of their fathers, the
nation was responsible to stone him (Deut. 13:1-5). On the
other hand, if his message was doctrinally sound, the miracle-
worker was to be accepted as coming with a message from God.
From the preponderance of Sadducees who were present at the
Sanhedrin meeting that morning, one can imagine what sort of
justice these proclaimers of Christ's resurrection could expect.

As the examination got underway, Peter and John were asked
to testify as to the power behind the miracle. Again Peter acts
as spokesman, and empowered by a fresh filling of the Holy
Spirit,[15] he admits the fact that a miracle of healing had been
performed. Furthermore, he testifies that the resurrected Jesus
Christ had furnished the power. He did not hesitate to lay the
blame for the crucifixion upon this very group, for it had been
they who had demanded his death and had delivered him to
Pilate.

To escape condemnation on the basis of Deuteronomy 13,
Peter must show that his teaching following the miracle did
not lead the people away from the God of their fathers. He
therefore associated Jesus with OT prophecy by showing that
he was the one spoken of in Psalm 118:22 as "the stone set at
nought." Jesus had applied this very passage to himself before
his death (Mark 12:10). Christ the living Stone (I Peter 2:4-8),
who had been rejected by these same leaders ("you builders"),
was the significant Stone in God's spiritual building of salvation
(note Ps. 118:21 for the mention of "salvation"). So far from
leading men into apostasy, Peter and John had been properly
expounding the OT through their proclamation of Jesus as the
Messiah.

2. *The Decision* (4:13-18)

This bold explanation from Peter amazed the Sanhedrin, coming as it did from such an unexpected source. Neither Peter nor
John had any technical, rabbinical training. In this sense they
were "unlearned,"[16] just as Jesus had been described by the

---

[15]The aorist passive participle *plēstheis* ("filled") points to an act performed upon him, rather than a continuing state.
[16]Greek: *agrammatoi*.

Jewish authorities earlier: "How knoweth this man letters, having never learned?" (John 7:15). Furthermore, they were mere laymen or private citizens, not officials or experts.[17] What amazed the council was that such a remarkable and lucid defense had come from these undistinguished men. (Certainly they did not conclude that Peter and John were illiterate and ignorant, as the unfortunate translation in KJV suggests.) They recognized that these men had been with Jesus, for he too had no rabbinical education and yet taught with such authority as to amaze his hearers (Matt. 7:28, 29; Luke 20:19-26). Perhaps they also remembered Peter and John from their presence with Jesus in the temple and at his trial (John 18:15, 16).

The presence of the lame man (had he been subpoenaed as a witness?) made the miracle undeniable; yet the Sanhedrin certainly did not wish to give approval to further apostolic preaching. The miracle had already achieved considerable publicity. Their only hope was to prevent the church from capitalizing on what had happened. They decided therefore to issue a restraining order prohibiting further speaking of any sort in the name of Christ. The threat was an absolute restriction: they must henceforth speak to no one regarding the message of Christ. It now became illegal to preach the gospel, whether in mass meeting or by personal encounter.

3. The Appeal (4:19-22)

When Peter and John were brought back to the courtroom to hear the verdict, they immediately appealed the decision to a higher court — to God himself. For Peter it was not an easy thing to take a position against the constituted authorities of his nation. He was no hot-eyed revolutionary itching for a chance to throw off the restraints of an unpopular government. He later wrote, "Submit yourselves to every ordinance of man for the Lord's sake: whether it be to the king, as supreme; or unto governors, as unto them that are sent by him for the punishment of evildoers, and for the praise of them that do well" (I Peter 2:13, 14). If there had been a way to obey the Sanhedrin without disobeying Christ's commission, the apostles would have done so. The Sanhedrin, however, left no way for compliance with

---

[17]Greek: *idiōtai*. See Heinrich Schlier, "Idiōtēs," *TDNT*, III, 215-217.

both them and Christ. Thus the obligation to obey human government is not absolute. If the government's orders are a violation of God's direct command, then the Christian must obey God. Following this principle cost the lives of many martyrs in the early centuries as well as in more recent times. It soon brought a reimprisonment of the apostles (Acts 5:17, 18). But as Peter later put it, "We must obey God rather than men" (Acts 5:29).

In spite of the apostles' clear statement that they could not comply with the order, the Sanhedrin released them with nothing more than repeated threats. What saved the apostles, humanly speaking, from more dire punishment was the public favor they enjoyed. Throughout the city the news of the miracle had spread, and politicians have always needed to take this factor into account when they planned their actions.

C. *The Outcome* (4:23-31)

Upon release from custody, Peter and John rejoined their fellow Christians[18] and reported what they had been told. The seriousness of this development was obvious, and it drove the group to prayer. One prominent feature in this prayer meeting was its emphasis upon the sovereignty of God. In times of great stress, it is no small comfort to recognize that God has not lost control. The very way in which God was addressed (the word translated "Lord" is *despota*, "absolute ruler") reflected the believers' faith that God who had created all things and had predicted with perfect accuracy the experiences of his Christ, was the One whose purposes were certain to be carried out. Thus they did not plead for the removal of the prospect of persecution, but were content merely to request that God would "behold their threatenings." Knowing that God was in control, they were content with his will, whatever form it might take. They asked for continued boldness to bear their witness, and prayed that God would authenticate their message with supernatural evidences during these foundational days.

Immediately they experienced the answer to their prayer.

---

[18]Since 5000-plus could not be accommodated in any building accessible to these Christians, Peter and John may have gone to the smaller group of leaders, perhaps in the upper room (1:13).

Their meeting place (the upper room?, Acts 1:13) was shaken (like the earthquake at Philippi?, Acts 16:26) as an outward indication of the Spirit's presence. Again they were filled with the Holy Spirit (see also Acts 2:4; 4:8), an operation of the Spirit which enabled them to perform their ministries with full effectiveness. Consequently, "they were continually involved in speaking[19] the word of God, the very activity regarding which they had prayed. The threat of the authorities could not frighten them, for they knew what Christ's command to them was, and they were relying upon the enablement provided by the Holy Spirit.

QUESTIONS FOR DISCUSSION
1. Why did the Christians continue worshipping at the Jewish temple?
2. In what way did Samuel prophesy about Christ?
3. Why were the Sadducees the first Jewish party to oppose the church?
4. In what sense were Peter and John unlearned and ignorant men?
5. Is it ever right to disobey the laws of one's government?

---

[19]Greek: *elaloun*. The imperfect tense denotes continuing activity.

Chapter 3

TROUBLE WITHIN AND WITHOUT
(Acts 4:32—5:42)

The first weeks after Pentecost were exciting ones for the church. The number of converts increased rapidly, and even unbelievers were favorably disposed toward the Christian movement (2:47; 4:21). The first opposition was relatively mild, resulting only in detention of Peter and John overnight and a threat against further preaching. When the apostles stated frankly that they would not be able to obey that order, nothing more was done to them and they were then released. After the church took the matter to God in prayer, they received immediate confirmation that God was with them, and their witness proceeded much as before (4:23-31). However, the early church was not perfect. There were troubles that surfaced within from time to time, and the opposition from her enemies on the outside soon increased in intensity.

I. TROUBLE WITHIN: ANANIAS AND SAPPHIRA (4:32—5:16)

A. *Fellowship in Heart and Goods* (4:32-37)

The church in Jerusalem was a beautiful example of Christian fellowship. It was no mere social club, but was an association based upon a true oneness of heart brought about by their common faith in Jesus Christ. Through the baptism of the Spirit at Pentecost (which subsequent believers experienced when they trusted Christ, Acts 2:38), they had become equal members of the body of Christ (I Cor. 12:13). This life-sharing union with Christ also created a spiritual fellowship with one another (I John 1:3; John 17:21).

This fellowship of heart and soul displayed itself in a willingness to share possessions. Their generosity sprang not from coercive legislation (as modern Socialists and Marxists demand) but from a true union of hearts made possible by regeneration.

This problem of poverty in the Jerusalem church was met by a voluntary selling of goods by the more wealthy Christians. We should not infer that every property owner sold every bit of property he owned, thus becoming poor himself. Rather as needs arose the rich sold possessions sufficient to alleviate the suffering of others. There is no record elsewhere in the NT of this specific procedure in caring for the poor within the church, although the implication is clear that it is the duty of the church to care for its own, whatever means may be adopted to do it (Acts 11:28, 29; I Tim. 5:3-16).

One whose generous act was the source of particular rejoicing was Joseph[1] Barnabas. It appears that the name "Barnabas" was given to him by the apostles in view of the great encouragement which he provided to the church. "Barnabas" means "son of encouragement,"[2] and reflects the common Jewish custom of using "son of" to denote a person's characteristics. The frequent OT expression "son of Belial" is a well-known example.

Several reasons may have prompted Luke's inclusion of this incident about Barnabas. The prominence of Barnabas in the later record of Acts adds special interest to all of his actions. It may also have been an important factor in the incident of Ananias and Sapphira which is next described. Finally, the fact that Barnabas was a Levite is an evidence that not all of those connected with the temple were implacable enemies of the gospel.

B. *The Episode of Ananias and Sapphira* (5:1-10)

Unhappily the fellowship enjoyed in the Jerusalem church was marred by the sad deceit of Ananias and Sapphira. Until this moment there had been no hint of friction or duplicity within the infant church. When it did appear, it occurred in the area of material possessions. "This present world" (see II Tim. 4:10) has exerted a strong attraction for God's people from the beginning until now. Examples such as these should warn every Christian of this ever-present danger.

Ananias and Sapphira were a husband and wife, recognized

[1]KJV: Joses.
[2]*huios paraklēseōs,* which can be translated as "son of consolation, exhortation, or encouragement."

as belonging to the Christian group. Their action is described as in contrast to Barnabas ("but," vs. 1). Perhaps they had noted the esteem with which the church regarded Barnabas, and desired similar recognition for themselves. They sold a piece of land,[3] retained a portion of the proceeds for themselves, and represented the part they presented to the apostles as being the entire purchase price. It should be noted that they were under no obligation to sell their property (Peter said, "While it remained, did it not remain thine own?"). And after they sold it, they had no need to give all of it or any of it to the church if they did not wish to ("after it was sold, was it not in thine own power?"). The whole procedure was their own choice.

Ananias came alone to present the money. Peter already knew of Ananias' guilt (whether by supernatural revelation or by more normal means), and told him that by his scheme he had lied to the Holy Spirit. It was the Spirit who had created the fellowship of one heart in the church, from which had come the sharing of goods. The action of Ananias was represented as an instance of this activity, when in reality it was not a response to the Spirit's leading at all. Thus he had lied to the Spirit by his deed.

Without a word Ananias dropped to the floor and died. Peter did not strike him dead nor call upon God to do so. He may have been as startled as the others. It was clear to the whole church, as well as to outsiders who heard of the incident, that God had intervened. Physical death was not unknown as a divine penalty (see Acts 12:23 and I Cor. 11:30-32 for later instances). Burial was cared for immediately. It was not customary to embalm in Palestine, and tombs were often in caves which had been previously prepared (note the burial of Jesus). Hence burial was usually carried out on the day of death. A period of three hours would have provided sufficient time.

Sapphira eventually entered the assembly, not aware of what had transpired. A great many more details would need to be known before one could discredit the account as improbable merely because of the burying of Ananias without Sapphira's knowledge. Perhaps she could not be located even

---

[3]Greek: *chōriou,* vs. 3.

though an attempt was made. Furthermore, the depositing of the body in a sepulchre would not prevent Sapphira from access to it later. More likely, since the death of Ananias was recognized as a divine judgment, this added a dimension to the whole incident that caused normal customs to be set aside. Peter may have understood that the same fate awaited Sapphira, and therefore it is possible that no attempt was even made to locate her.

Peter asked Sapphira whether the property had been sold for the precise amount brought to him by Ananias. When she said, "Yea, for so much," she added an open lie to the previous duplicity. Her guilt was fully as great as her husband's. Consequently, she too was struck down by God on the spot, and was buried by the same young men who had just buried Ananias.

Were Ananias and Sapphira pretended believers whose falsity was finally unmasked? Or were they genuine Christians whose death was a discipline from God? In favor of the former explanation is the undeniable fact that they did not act as true Christians should. Furthermore, they are obviously contrasted with Barnabas and the others who were of "one heart and one soul" (4:32). However, there are a number of factors which suggest that they may have been Christians who were disciplined by God. (1) Acts 4:32 indicates that all who engaged in the community of goods were believers, and though Ananias and Sapphira are contrasted with Barnabas, there is nothing to indicate that they were not understood as members of the "multitude of them that believed." (2) Satan can energize saved people (David, I Chron. 21:1; Peter, Matt. 16:21-23; Christians in general, I Peter 5:8, 9). (3) Physical death is a discipline applied to some Christians (I Cor. 11:30-32). (4) The fact of lying to the Holy Spirit is more easily understood of Christians indwelt by the Spirit than of unbelievers who have no relation to God and certainly have no special relationship to the Holy Spirit.

If they were Christians, their death had a value in not causing others to be led astray, nor in allowing them to continue in a course of sin. God's attitude toward sin was clearly revealed, and the purity of the infant church was maintained. Although

physical death as a discipline for Christians is mentioned elsewhere in the NT (I Cor. 11:30-32; I John 5:16), it apparently
did not always occur as suddenly and dramatically as this instance in Acts 5. It must be remembered that in the early days
of the church many things happened as examples and guides
which do not necessarily recur throughout her history (for

Fig. 5. Solomon's Porch is the colonnaded walkway on the far side of
the temple enclosure in this model. It became the meeting place of the
early Jerusalem Christians. Photo by the author

instance, tongues of fire, raising of the dead). Nevertheless,
God may still use this means of discipline at times. It is a
sobering thought, one that deserves due consideration by God's
people.

C. *The Continued Growth of the Church* (5:11-16)

Even though a serious matter had just occurred within the
confines of the Christian group, God's way of dealing with it
preserved the integrity of the church, and fostered genuine
growth. The first result was a healthy fear on the part of the

church as well as outsiders. It had been made very clear that this movement was more than just another religious party. Supernatural power had been involved not only in the miraculous phenomena at the outset on Pentecost, but was still very much present. Purity of life was of great importance and the judgment just exercised had a sobering effect upon all who learned what happened. Verse 11 contains the first mention of the word "church" *(ekklēsia)* in Acts.[4]

The purified church demonstrated the power of God in its labors and contacts. The headquarters for their public gatherings was Solomon's Porch, the colonnade along the east wall of the temple grounds. It was an ideal spot for their meetings, being at the religious center of the city and providing in that vast concourse an opportunity for multitudes of interested people to learn of the church without having to commit themselves prematurely. The performance of signs and wonders by the apostles in this public setting gave the greatest possible exposure to the Christian movement.

Continued conversions in Jerusalem also characterized these days. Multitudes of men and women believed, and were added by the miracle of new birth to the life-sharing fellowship with the Lord and with one another.[5] The reference to "the rest" in verse 13 is capable of several explanations. Some have understood "the rest" as the ordinary believers (in distinction from the apostles) who feared to usurp the prerogatives of the apostles ("daring to join himself to them") after seeing the judgment meted out to Ananias and Sapphira through Peter. However, the sin of Ananias was not an attempt to usurp apostolic authority. A more likely explanation sees "the rest" as unbelievers (in distinction from the believers of vs. 12) who, even though admiring and respecting the Christians ("magnified them"), did not dare to become affiliated with the church because they had learned to fear what could happen to halfhearted

---

[4]The Western text contained *ekklēsia* at 2:47, and this found its way into the received text and KJV. The older and generally more reliable manuscripts do not support its inclusion in this earlier reference.

[5]The Greek text of verse 14 is capable of being rendered in two ways: (1) "Believers were the more added to the Lord" (so KJV, ASV), or (2) "There were the more added to them, ones believing the Lord" (so ASV margin).

faith. Thus these multitudes of new believers were not the product of a mere membership drive. The statement may also imply that as a general practice the unbelievers actually left the Christians alone and undisturbed for their meetings. They were free to meet in this public place and yet be relatively isolated so as to carry out their worshipping and teaching activities. Of the signs and wonders performed by the apostles, some of the most spectacular involved physical healings and demon exorcisms. Beneficiaries included not only residents of Jerusalem, but people from surrounding areas as well. The desire of the people to be contacted by Peter's shadow for healing was not necessarily superstition, for a woman once desired to touch Jesus' garment and yet he said to her, "Thy faith hath made thee whole" (Matt. 9:20-22). God was working through Peter, and it made little difference whether the instrument was the hem of a garment, clay and spittle, the pool of Siloam, or the shadow of an apostle. It was God's will which provided the power.

II. TROUBLE WITHOUT: MORE PERSECUTION (5:17-42)

A. *The Twelve Arrested* (5:17-26)

Once again the temple authorities were aroused against the apostles (cf. 4:1, 2). The high priest[6] and his associates, all of whom were Sadducees and thus opposed in principle to the Christian movement, were moved to take steps to silence the apostolic preaching. Earlier the Sanhedrin had commanded no further teaching in the name of Christ (4:18), but their order had been disobeyed (as in fact Peter and John had told them it would be). Now the authorities were consumed with jealousy.[7] Perhaps they feared that this disregarding of their orders might spread and bring all their power into jeopardy. They may also have been envious of their popularity, for the apostles were being respected and sought after throughout the city as men with a message from God. Consequently, they arrested all twelve of the apostles (the earlier occasion had involved only

---

[6]This high priest was presumably Caiaphas, who remained in office until A.D. 36.

[7]Greek: *zēlou*, jealousy, envy.

Peter and John, Acts 4:1-3), and placed them in the public jail overnight.

During the night, however, an angel[8] opened the prison doors, and instructed the twelve to return to the temple and continue speaking to the people. The question might be asked whether the angelic release was not useless since the twelve were promptly re-arrested just a few hours later. A careful reflection on this narrative will show, however, that the re-arrested apostles were in a different position than after their first arrest (notice vs. 26). They were handled gingerly, and the speech of Gamaliel brought their release. The outcome could conceivably have been quite different if God had not intervened.

In the morning the Sanhedrin[9] convened to consider for the second time the problem posed by the continuation of apostolic preaching. The inability of the officers to produce the twelve prisoners brought considerable consternation. When the apostles' whereabouts were eventually reported to the Sanhedrin, there occurred a quiet re-arrest. In spite of the fact that their preaching was a clear violation of the Sanhedrin's command (4:18, 21), the apostles were handled with extreme caution by their captors. The soldiers feared that they might be pelted with stones by the crowds which still esteemed the apostles highly.

B. *The Twelve on Trial* (5:27-40a)

The high priest, in his regular position as president of the Sanhedrin, conducted the investigation. Two things specifically formed the basis of his complaint. First, the Sanhedrin's previous command had been flagrantly disobeyed. This should have been no surprise, however, for Peter and John had clearly stated that they would be continuing their preaching (4:18, 20). Second, the Sanhedrin was being blamed for the death of Jesus. This sensitivity of the council to having "this man's blood upon us" is strange in the light of the statements made not many weeks before by the multitudes who were urged on by these

---

[8]The Greek text has no article with *angelos*.

[9]The two terms "council" (*sunedrion*) and "senate" (*gerousian*) do not denote two separate bodies (for which there is no clear evidence). The second term should be understood as appositional or epexegetical.

priests, "His blood be on us, and on our children" (Matt. 27:20, 25). These charges by the Sanhedrin reveal how effective the apostolic preaching had been. Jerusalem had been quite well evangelized, and the Sanhedrin was actually becoming alarmed.

Peter acted as spokesman for the apostles in giving their defense. He mentioned first that God's orders must take precedence over the Sanhedrin in cases where the two conflict. Now it was God who had raised Jesus from the dead, the one whom these very council members had condemned to death. God had not only raised Jesus from the dead but had exalted him to his own right hand, the position of honor and authority. This Jesus was established by God as the Prince and Savior, whose purpose was to bring Israel to repentance and salvation. To that end Jesus had given the apostles the task of being witnesses, and God had provided them with the Holy Spirit as their source of power. This was why they felt compelled to disobey the silencing order of the Sanhedrin, for to comply would have been to disobey the command of their Savior, whose program was clearly that of God Himself.

This defense, of course, sounded blasphemous to many in the Sanhedrin. Their plans to kill the twelve were vitiated, however, by the counsel of Gamaliel who mollified the Sadducean majority by a persuasive speech. Gamaliel was a highly respected Pharisee, grandson of the famous Hillel, and the teacher of Saul of Tarsus (22:3). Being a Pharisee he would not wish to see the Sadducees make political capital out of ridding the nation of an alleged threat to its religious purity. If it be wondered why the Sadduccees, being the majority group in the Sanhedrin, would let their designs be altered by a Pharisee, perhaps the comment by Josephus, himself a first-century Jew, may be enlightening. He wrote regarding the Sadducees:

> They accomplish practically nothing, however. For whenever they assume some office, though they submit unwillingly and perforce, yet submit they do to the formulas of the Pharisees, since, otherwise the masses would not tolerate them.[10]

Gamaliel's counsel urged the Sanhedrin to adopt a milder policy toward the apostles, at least for the present. He argued that if this were merely another human movement, it would

_____
[10]*Antiquities* XVIII.1.4.

fade away in due time as countless others had. On the other hand, if this new doctrine were of God, the Sanhedrin would surely not want to take a contrary position, for that would be neither laudable nor successful.

He cited two instances from Jewish history to show the practicality of his advice. The mention of Theudas poses a problem inasmuch as Josephus also refers to a rebel leader by this name but one who appeared on the scene during the governorship of Cuspius Fadus (A.D. 44-46).[11] This was many years subsequent to Gamaliel's speech. Furthermore, Gamaliel places Theudas prior to Judas, whose sedition occurred at the time of the enrolment in A.D. 6, whereas Josephus places him later than Judas. Inasmuch as Josephus' *Antiquities* was not published until in the A.D. 90's, and Acts was almost certainly written much earlier (see Introduction), it cannot be demonstrated that Luke had read Josephus and had miscopied from him. Rather, we may conclude either that Josephus erred (it would not have been the only time) or more probably that there were two Theudases in view. This was an abbreviation of several very common names, and there was an almost incredible number of insurrections during this period. Josephus himself spoke of 10,000 disorders, 10,000 rebels, and of 2,000 who were crucified for revolting prior to the enrolment of A.D. 6.[12] Hence the Theudas mentioned by Gamaliel could well have been a different person from the one cited by Josephus. The mention of Judas of Galilee provides no problem, and is fully confirmed by references in Josephus.[13]

The soundness of Gamaliel's advice may be questiond. It is, of course, true that ultimately God's program will emerge victorious, and human schemes will perish. It is also true that many times hasty action is foolish because it is taken before all the facts are known. Nevertheless, one cannot always judge from short-term results whether an enterprise is God's work or not, and we may not have time enough to wait for the final issue. The measure is not the pragmatic one of apparent success, but its conformity to the revealed will of God. Present temporary

---

[11] *Ibid.*, XX.5.1.
[12] *Ibid.*, XVII.10.4, 10.
[13] *Ibid.*, XVIII.1.1; X.5.2.

failures (or successes) may not be final. It is possible, however, that Gamaliel's point was: since the movements of Theudas and Judas collapsed when they were slain, the Christian movement should also collapse shortly if it were only human, inasmuch as Jesus had been killed.

C. *The Twelve Released* (5:40b-42)

The Sanhedrin was persuaded by the advice of Gamaliel, whether it was sound or not. They repeated their previous threats against further preaching, and ordered the twelve to be beaten before release. The usual beating consisted of forty stripes, lessened by one to avoid accidentally exceeding the legal limit (Deut. 25:3; II Cor. 11:24). This was the first actual suffering experienced by the Christians. The beating did not frighten them nor discourage them from continued witnessing. Both in the temple and in various houses they continued their ministry of instructing and evangelizing. Neither trouble within nor trouble without could stop the work which God had started.

QUESTIONS FOR DISCUSSION

1. Were Ananias and Sapphira saved people?
2. Does God discipline people in the church today?
3. What are some ways in which people lie to the Holy Spirit?
4. Was Gamaliel's advice a sound principle to follow in determining the will of God?

Chapter 4

SERVING AND SUFFERING
(Acts 6, 7)

The early months of the Christian church were filled with excitement. Tremendous growth, supernatural displays, and moments of high drama characterized the new movement. But clouds were darkening on the horizon, and the church had already begun to experience something of the troubles that would be her lot. The believers had recently found that worldly concerns could affect those within their number. She was yet to learn that mundane matters can cause problems not just in isolated cases (as Ananias and Sapphira) but to a degree that the whole church becomes affected. The Christian life involves not only participating in great spiritual victories, it includes much of ordinary routine, of matters physical and organizational. Upon occasion it brings suffering even to the loss of life. To the credit of the Jerusalem church, she learned these lessons well.

I. THE CHOOSING OF THE SEVEN (6:1-7)

A. *The Need* (6:1, 2)

Luke mentions at least three factors which caused the problem confronting the church at this time. First, there had been a huge increase in the number of converts, and this vast influx of new members brought certain practical problems. The last total given in Acts was five thousand men (4:4), but multitudes had believed since that count (5:14). In spite of official opposition, the populace of Jerusalem continued to hold the disciples in high regard (5:26), and converts continued to be made.

Second, the Jerusalem believers were of two groups, and there had been friction between these groups since long before the Christian era. Both groups were Jews. The "Hebrews" were native Palestinian Jews who spoke Aramaic and used the Hebrew Scriptures. The "Hellenists" were Greek-cultured Jews, many of whom had returned to Palestine in their later years.

These spoke Greek regularly, used the LXX as their Scripture, and were sometimes resented by their Hebrew brethren. In the second century B.C., I Maccabees described with much disapproval those Jews who adopted Greek customs:

> In those days came there forth out of Israel transgressors of the law, and persuaded many, saying, Let us go and make a covenant with the Gentiles that are round about us; for since we were parted from them many evils have befallen us. And the saying was good in their eyes. And certain of the people were forward herein and went to the king, and he gave them license to do after the ordinances of the Gentiles. And they built a place of exercise in Jerusalem according to the laws of the Gentiles; and they made themselves uncircumcised, and forsook the holy covenant, and joined themselves to the Gentiles, and sold themselves to do evil. (1:11-15)

Although these Hellenists in Acts were not apostates like those in Maccabean times, memories are long in the middle east, and suspicions may still have lingered among their descendants in both cultures. Friction between the groups erupted in the church over the problem of caring for the widows. When distribution to those in need was made under apostolic supervision (2:45; 4:34-37), the Hellenist group felt that their widows were being neglected. Inasmuch as they thought that it was their widows as a group, apparently they must have felt it was deliberate. The complaint may have been justified (the apostles never denied it, and took immediate steps to rectify the problem), but the oversight must certainly have been accidental.

The third factor contributing to the problem was the specific task that was the apostles' prime responsibility. That was their duty to devote themselves to ministering the word in preaching and teaching. To administer the distribution of goods was a burden that had mushroomed in recent weeks. Their organization had not kept pace with the rapid expansion of the church.

B. *The Method* (6:3-6)

The apostles suggested to the church that seven men should be chosen to care for this task. These seven would free the apostles for their main task of ministering the word of God and spending time in prayer. The seven were to be Christian men ("among you") who had the respect of the group, and who showed themselves to be controlled by the Holy Spirit. Furthermore, they should have the mental capacity to handle the task properly. Real discretion needed to be exercised in choosing these men, for their task would require honesty, tact, sympathy, and considerable practical wisdom.

Although these seven are not called "deacons," cognate words do occur in the chapter three times (*diakoniāi*, vss. 1, 4; *diakonein*, vs. 2). Inasmuch as the epistles indicate the existence of officers called deacons who appear to be secondary to the leaders of the church (Phil. 1:1; I Tim. 3), and since there is no other place where their ministry is described, it seems very possible that their origin should be traced to the Seven.

It is worth noting that the expression "serve tables" may not demand that we imagine the apostles as caterers or table waiters in the restaurant sense. "Tables"[1] often denoted "banks," because moneylenders sat at tables to conduct their business. The word is used in that sense in Luke 19:23 and Matthew 21:12. The apostles may have meant that they should not leave their ministry of the word to serve as bankers or money-dispensers.

The congregation then selected seven men to assume this task. The men who were chosen all had Greek names, and it is sometimes asserted that all were of the Hellenist group — surely a gracious gesture to the complainers if that were so. However, many Palestinian Jews had Greek names (for example, the apostle Philip), so this feature is not to be pressed. Nevertheless, one of them was actually a gentile by birth — Nicolas, a proselyte to Judaism who came from Antioch. The Seven were placed before the apostles for official installation into their position. After prayer for God's blessing, hands were laid on them, symbolizing probably the blessing of God[2] as well as their official identification as the duly appointed functionaries.[3] Nothing mystical was conveyed by the action, however, for they were "full of the spirit" prior to their being chosen.

C. *The Outcome* (6:7)

When the new organization was effected, the results were

---

[1]Greek: *trapezai*.

[2]Imposition of hands was the symbol of blessing in such instances as Matt. 19:13-15 and Gen. 48:14-20.

[3]See Num. 8:10, 11 for an instance of this usage of the rite.

immediate and positive. The word of God was disseminated more effectively because the apostles had more time to devote to its proclamation. The number of disciples experienced another remarkable increase. Among the converts were many priests. These were hardly the Sadducean aristocrats, but were most likely common priests, many of whom were godly men who were open to the gospel (cf. Zacharias, Luke 1).

II. THE MINISTRY OF STEPHEN (6:8-15)

A. *Among the People* (6:8)

In addition to his service as a ministrant to the widows, Stephen was active as a witness among the people in Jerusalem. The grace[4] and power of God were upon him, enabling him to perform outstanding miracles which produced wonderment (*terata*) as well as proofs (*sēmeia*) of God's presence.

B. *In the Synagogue* (6:9-12a)

Stephen did not confine his witness to Solomon's Porch (5:12), but contacted Jews in the synagogue as well. It is not certain how many synagogues are referred to in verse 9. Guesses have ranged from one to five, and the grammar of the text is not conclusive. "Libertines" in all probability means "freedmen," and may refer to former slaves (perhaps from the four cities or provinces mentioned) who apparently had their own synagogue in Jerusalem. Stephen himself was probably a Hellenist, and perhaps was a member of the synagogue (or one of the synagogues) in view.

In 1913-14 an inscription was found during excavations on Ophel in Jerusalem that may have been a part of the "Synagogue of the Freedmen." George Ernest Wright translates the text as follows:

> Theodotus son of Vettenus, priest and synagogue-president, son of a synagogue-president and grandson of a synagogue-president, has built the synagogue for the reading of the Law and the teaching of the Comandments, and (he has built) the hostelry and the chambers and the cisterns of water in order to provide lodgings for those from abroad

---

[4] A literal rendering of the text describes him as one "full of grace and power."

Fig. 6. Theodotos Inscription, from the ruins of a first century synagogue in Jerusalem which may have been the Synagogue of the Libertines where Stephen preached. By courtesy of the Israel Department of Antiquities and Museums

who need them — (the synagogue) which his fathers and elders and Simonides had founded.[5]

It is thought to be the synagogue of the Freedmen because the Roman family name Vettenus suggests that the donor must have been a Jewish freedman who had come from Italy.

Failure to refute Stephen's preaching brought the use of false witnesses who were procured to charge him with religious blasphemy. This caused the loss of public favor ("they stirred up the people") which the Christians had previously enjoyed (5:13, 26; 4:21), and was a most significant factor in subsequent days.

C. *Before the Sanhedrin* (6:12b-15)

Called before the Sanhedrin, Stephen was charged with blasphemy on three counts: (1) Blasphemy against God (vs. 11). (2) Blasphemy against the temple[6] (vs. 13). (3) Blas-

---

[5]*Biblical Archaeology* (Philadelphia, 1962 ed.), p. 240.

[6]Ancient manuscript evidence varies at vs. 13 in referring to the temple either as "the holy place" (*tou topou tou hagiou*) or as "this holy place" (*tou topou tou hagiou toutou*). If the latter is correct, it could imply that the Sanhedrin was actually meeting within the temple precincts.

phemy against the Mosaic Law (vss. 11, 13). The charge of
temple blasphemy was based upon a perversion of a statement
by Jesus, which misstatement was used against our Lord at his
trial (Matt. 26:60, 61). The true words of Jesus are recorded
in John 2:19, "You destroy this temple [not "I will destroy"],
and in three days I will raise it up," and, of course, he wasn't
referring to the building on the temple mount at all.

The enigmatic statement that Stephen's face had the appearance of an angel's may indicate a supernatural glow, similar to
that of Moses when he came down from the mount (Exod.
34:29-35). The vision of Christ which he received later in the
council makes the comparison with Moses somewhat similar,
although the unusual appearance of Stephen's face seems to
have begun before the vision, whereas in the case of Moses it
came afterward. Saul of Tarsus was probably Luke's source
for this report.

III. THE SPEECH OF STEPHEN (7:1-53)

The high priest Caiaphas[7] was the presiding officer of the
Sanhedrin. He asked Stephen how he would plead to these
charges of blasphemy. Stephen's response was not a direct
answer to the question, and yet it did provide a defense by
showing unmistakably what Stephen's attitude was toward the
God of Israel, the OT law, and the temple — the three areas in
which he was accused of blasphemy.

To the Western reader this speech seems to be a strange sort
of defense for a man on trial for his life. It must be remembered,
however, that the Jews were fond of historical retrospection,
and with good reason. In view of the remarkable dealings of
God with their nation in the past, it is small wonder that in
times of adversity Jews often found comfort in tracing their
history to see God's mercy, and to find encouragement for
greater trust. Psalms 78 and 107 are other examples of this
practice. Stephen, however, was not trying to find encouragement for himself, but was endeavoring to show how the
Christian message was fully consistent with and the culmination of OT revelation.

---

[7]Caiaphas remained in office until A.D. 36.

Stephen was obviously a man of learning. His speech must have made a deep impression upon the still-unconverted Saul of Tarsus. Perhaps the memory of it was one of the "goads" which was prodding his conscience enroute to Damascus (26:14). The first sermon of Saul (called Paul by that time) whose content is fully recorded in Acts is strikingly like Stephen's (13:16-41). The concepts of Stephen regarding the proper attitude toward the temple are similar to those expressed later in the Epistle to the Hebrews, where the tabernacle is emphasized as being only an earthly copy, and not the ultimate reality. Stephen's accusers seem to have forgotten that fact.

A comparison of the historical details cited by Stephen with the OT record reveals some difficulties.[8] Some would explain the discrepancies by asserting that Luke has given an inerrant record of what Stephen said (errors and all). This does not satisfy all interpreters, however. The emphasis in Acts upon Stephen's control by the Holy Spirit and the Divine approval upon his ministry and upon this testimony before the Sanhedrin (6:5, 15; 7:55) makes it extremely doubtful that this speech was saturated with errors of fact. A careful study of the data indicates that harmonization of the alleged discrepancies is presently possible in most cases, and impossible in none if we are willing to delay judgment until more data is available.

A. *God's Activity with Abraham and the Patriarchs* (7:1-19)

In answer to the high priest's question, Stephen began his response by emphasizing the God of glory who revealed himself to Abraham, and continued to lead in the affairs of the patriarchs in order to accomplish his purpose. It should have been clear to the Sanhedrin that Stephen was absolutely orthodox in his faith and respect for the God of Israel. The speech also stressed the fact that historically God had to contend continually with a disobedient people, even among the patriarchs who sold Joseph to Egypt. According to Stephen, the important thing was to see God's purposes, not man's actions which were often sinful and contradictory to God's will. The treatment of

---

[8]R. B. Rackham, for instance, lists 15 historical problems. Some of them are very minor, however, consisting not of contradictions but of additions to the record, *The Acts of the Apostles,* pp. 99-102.

Joseph by his Hebrew brothers should have been a pointed reminder of the way Jesus had been dealt with by the Jewish nation.

Certain historical problems in this portion of the speech deserve comment.

1. The call of Abraham is placed by Stephen in Mesopotamia, before he moved to Haran. Yet the content of the call is stated by Stephen in the words of Genesis 12:1, which appears to place the event in Haran. However, Genesis 15:7 also indicates that Abraham left Ur because of God's action,[9] and Genesis 11:31 and 12:1 do not contradict this. Either we should understand that the call in Ur was repeated in Haran, or else that there was only one call, but it was in Ur and Genesis 12:1 refers to that call.

2. The death of Abraham's father Terah is placed before Abraham's departure from Haran. A comparison of the data in Genesis (11:26, 32; 12:4) seems to indicate that Terah lived another 60 years *after* Abraham left. Genesis states that Terah was 70 when he fathered his oldest son, presumably Abraham (11:26). Since Abraham was 75 when he left Haran (12:4), Terah would have been 145. Yet Terah did not die till he was 205 (11:32). The best solution seems to be that Abraham was not the oldest son of Terah, but was named first because he was the most prominent (11:26).[10] If Abraham were born when Terah was 130, the figures are harmonized.

3. Israel's bondage in Egypt is stated as being 400 years. Exodus 12:40 states the time in Egypt as being 430 years (so Gal. 3:17). The LXX says 215 years. Genesis 15:13 gives the time of the affliction as 400 years. Paul in his sermon at Antioch uses the figure 450 years to include the time of Israel in Egypt, the wilderness, and the period of conquest (Acts 13:19, 20). For an extended treatment of this complex problem, the reader should consult specialized studies on this question.[11] Stephen

---

[9]Josephus says the same thing, *Antiquities* I.7.1.

[10]F. F. Bruce, however rejects this as an improbable expedient, and speculates that Stephen had a Greek version of Genesis not presently extant which supported his data, *The Book of the Acts*, pp. 146, 147 footnote.

[11]See Harold W. Hoehner, "The Duration of the Egyptian Bondage," *Bibliotheca Sacra* CXXVI, 504 (October-December, 1969), pp. 306-316;

may be understood as indebted particularly to Genesis 15:13, and the 400 years should be understood either as referring specifically to the bondage portion of the sojourn in Egypt, or else as a round number for the sojourn (which more precisely was 430 years).

4. The total number of Jacob's family is said to be seventy-five persons, but Genesis gives the figure as seventy. The number was arrived at as follows: Genesis 46:26 gives a total of sixty-six as those who accompanied Jacob to Egypt, omitting Jacob himself, Joseph, and the two sons of Joseph, and of course not counting any wives or daughters. Genesis 46:27 apparently adds four (Jacob, Joseph, and Joseph's two sons) to arrive at the total of seventy. The same total is given in Exodus 1:5. The LXX, however, uses the figure seventy-five in these latter two references.

The difference was caused by a slightly different method of computation. In Genesis 46:26, 27, the LXX adds sixty-six and nine to get seventy-five (where the Hebrew Masoretic text has added sixty-six and four). Instead of adding two sons of Joseph, the LXX mentions nine sons.[12] It apparently includes the two sons (Ephraim and Manasseh), five grandsons, and two other grandsons who died (Num. 26:28-37; I Chron. 7:14-23). In view of the fact that sons and even grandsons were counted in the figure sixty-six, it would not be inconsistent to count sons of Ephraim and Manasseh since they became tribal heads in place of their father Joseph. This is also in harmony with the Jewish way of regarding descendants as already present in the loins of the father, even before they were born.[13] Stephen apparently cited the LXX figure which really was not an error, but computed the total differently by including five people which the Masoretic text did not.

5. The burial of Jacob and his sons is stated with marked differences from the OT. Stephen seems to say that Jacob and

Jack R. Riggs, "The Length of Israel's Sojourn in Egypt," *Grace Journal*, XII, 1 (Winter, 1971), pp. 18-35.

[12]LXX: *huioi de Iōsēph hoi genomenoi autōi en gēi Aiguptōi psuchai ennea* (Gen. 46:27).

[13]Note this concept in Heb. 7:9 (Abraham-Levi), and I Cor. 15:22 (Adam — all men).

his sons were buried in the tomb that Abraham bought from
the sons of Hamor. The OT states that Jacob was buried at
Hebron in the cave of Machpelah which Abraham bought from
Ephron (Gen. 23:1-20; 49:29-33; 50:13). It is possible to
understand Acts 7:16 to refer only to the sons of Jacob, not
Jacob himself, and to this the OT offers no contradiction, for
it says nothing about the burial place of the sons. The OT
reports, as does Stephen, that Joseph was buried at Shechem
(Gen. 33:19; Josh. 24:32), but it relates the purchase to Jacob,
not Abraham. Some explain this as an instance of telescoping
in which two events are compressed into one. The expanded
thought would be: Abraham and Jacob bought burial sites
from Ephron in Hebron and Hamor in Shechem.[14] Others suggest that Abraham actually may have made the original purchase
and Jacob later had to re-purchase the plot.[15] Abraham was in
Shechem, and must have needed to acquire some property to
erect his altar (Gen. 12:6, 7).

B. *God's Activity through Moses* (7:20-43)

In his tracing of Israel's history, Stephen devotes considerable
time to the experience of Moses. This was one of the areas in
which he stood accused. By this testimony Stephen showed
that he was no blasphemer of the Mosaic Law, for his belief in
the ministry of Moses and in the divine circumstances involved
in the giving of the law was in the best traditions of his people.
Nevertheless, he reminded the Sanhedrin that Israel had generally resisted God's dealings and God's leader. As in the case
of Joseph, so it was with Moses — the people rejected him even
though God had indicated him as their deliverer. It was not
Stephen who was the blasphemer, for he had accepted Moses'
prophecy about the coming Prophet (vs. 37). It was the Sanhedrin who had rejected.

Stephen's quotation of Amos 5:27, "I will carry you away
beyond Babylon," differs from the OT. Both the Hebrew text

---

[14]See J. A. Alexander, *Commentary on the Acts of the Apostles* (Grand
Rapids, reprint edition, 1956), pp. 269, 269; F. F. Bruce, *The Book of the
Acts*, p. 149n.
[15]See J. Rawson Lumby, *The Acts of the Apostles* in Cambridge Greek
Testament for Schools and Colleges (Cambridge, 1885), pp. 164, 165.

and the LXX say "Damascus." The prophet Amos was fore-
telling the exile of the northern kingdom under the Assyrians
which would take them beyond Damascus. More than a century
later, the southern kingdom was captured because of her similar
disobedience to God and was deported to Babylon. Stephen has
merely substituted this phrase in order to use this Scripture to
cover the judgment of God on the entire nation.

C. God's Activity through David and Solomon (7:44-53)

In this section Stephen shows his attitude about the physical
temple, and reminds his hearers that a superstitious reverence
for the building was contrary to the attitude of Solomon himself who had built an even more splendid edifice than the one
of Stephen's day. The original tabernacle was the only edifice
which God had actually ordered. This tabernacle was brought
into Canaan under Joshua.[16] When finally a permanent temple
was built by Solomon, it was Solomon himself who declared the
omnipresence of God (I Kings 8:27), and stated that God could
not really be contained in a physical building.

Applying these historical precedents to his audience, Stephen
accused them of having the same rebellious nature as their
fathers. Their ancestors had persecuted the prophets who foretold Christ's coming, and when Christ came this Sanhedrin had
killed him. Their hardness of heart showed them to be no
better spiritually than uncircumcised gentiles.

IV. THE STONING OF STEPHEN (7:54-60)

The Sanhedrin was incensed by Stephen's accusations (after
all, he was supposed to be the defendant, not the prosecutor).
They apparently interrupted his message before he was able to
speak much of Jesus and the resurrection. Nevertheless, God
granted him a vision of the glorified Jesus, and this he promptly
announced to his judges. The Sanhedrin erupted in a frenzy,
and took Stephen outside the city where they stoned him to
death. Stephen followed the example of his Savior in praying
for his slayers, as well as for himself. Part of the answer to his

---

[16]The names Jesus and Joshua are simply variant English spellings of the
same Hebrew and Greek terms. In this passage the OT Joshua is meant.

prayer was the conversion of Saul, whose presence at the scene
was noted by Luke.

Was this a legal execution by the Sanhedrin? Those who
think so point to its performance outside the city (Lev. 24:14;
Num. 15:35), and the fact that the witnesses did the stoning
(Deut. 17:7). The mention of Saul as "consenting" (8:1) might
possibly be understood as participating in a formal vote. There
are good reasons, however, for understanding this as more of a
lynching than a legal act. Verse 57 reads more like a spontaneous
outburst than a formal vote. Furthermore, Jewish law at this
time specified that capital cases must have a second trial at least
one day later. In addition, Rome did not allow the Sanhedrin to
execute prisoners (note the case of Jesus), and it is difficult to
imagine how the Sanhedrin expected to avoid serious trouble
with Rome if this were a deliberate and formal execution.
Finally, the sort of burial given to Stephen (8:2) was not allowed after legal executions.[17] It seems best, therefore, to regard
it as mob violence, with the Sanhedrin forming the mob which
took the life of the first Christian to seal his witness with his
blood.

QUESTIONS FOR DISCUSSION

1. What did the early church understand its responsibility to be regarding
   social problems?
2. What was Stephen trying to prove in his speech?
3. Can you find any parallels between Israel's past history and Jewish
   attitudes in Stephen's day?
4. What are some of the values of studying OT history?

---

[17]"Tract Sanhedrin," Chapter VI, Mishna VI, *The Babylonian Talmud*
(Boston, 1918) trans. Michael L. Rodkinson, VIII, 126-148.

**THE EARLY GROWTH:
PALESTINE AND SYRIA
Acts 8 — 12**

Chapter 5

PHILIP, SAUL, AND PETER
(Acts 8, 9)

The death of Stephen marked the end of phase one of the Christian movement. That phase had seen Jerusalem thoroughly saturated with the gospel. The city had by no means become predominantly Christian,[1] but it had been confronted with the message of Christ on every level of its society. Priests, Sanhedrin, Hellenists, and Hebrews had all heard the forthright proclamation of the resurrection of Christ, and thousands had responded with faith. The ministry of Stephen, however, provided the polarization which meant that things could no longer go on as before. The loss of popular favor (6:12) removed the chief restraint against the violent hatred among the Sanhedrin. An outbreak of city-wide persecution was an almost inevitable consequence. All it needed was a leader and the spark to set it off.

I. THE MINISTRY OF PHILIP (8:1-40)

A. *The Scattering of the Jerusalem Church* (8:1-4)

Stephen's death supplied the spark. Saul of Tarsus provided the leadership. Formerly the Sadducees had been the primary opponents of the Christian movement (4:1; 5:17), and the Pharisees and adopted a somewhat mediating position (5:34). Now Saul the Pharisee (23:6) abandoned the milder stance of his teacher Gamaliel and engaged in an energetic campaign of persecution. The mention of his name three times in this section (7:58; 8:1, 3) indicates his prominence in these events, and the coupling of the cessation of the persecution with the conversion

---

[1]Estimates vary as to the population of Jerusalem during these days.(C. C. McCown gives the figure as about 100,000, "The Density of Population in Ancient Palestine," *Journal of Biblical Literature,* Vol. LXVI, Part IV [December, 1947], p. 436.) To this should be compared Luke's computation of Christians as 5,000 men (Acts 4:4), with multitudes added later (5:14; 6:1; 6:7).

of Saul strongly suggests that he was the prime mover in this outbreak.

This persecution resulted in the Christians being driven from Jerusalem to the neighboring regions of Judea and Samaria. Although it is stated that "all" were scattered from Jerusalem except the apostles, it cannot be concluded that this was permanent exclusion. In subsequent years we find the church still existing in Jerusalem (9:26; 11:1-2; 11:22; 12:1-5; 15:4). Why were the apostles untouched in this attack? They had been the chief victims earlier (4:1-3; 5:18). Perhaps they determined to remain at their posts at all costs and God protected them. It may have been, however, that the special objects of this persecution were the Hellenist Christians (and, of course, the apostles would all have been Hebrews).[2] The whole uprising had begun through Stephen's synagogue preaching among the Hellenists (6:9). Furthermore, in 11:19, 20 specific mention is made that some of those who were driven out by this persecution were Hellenists.

Stephen's burial was performed by certain "devout men." This term is used every other time in the NT to denote either pious Jews (Luke 2:25; Acts 2:5) or else a Christian Jew whose piety was described in relation to the Mosaic law (Acts 22:12). In view of the fact that the Christians were the objects of attack, it may be that his burial was carried out by some of his Jewish friends who deplored his tragic death, and saw to it that the customary rites were observed. This burial also indicates that Stephen's death was not a legal execution.[3]

B. The Evangelization of Samaria (8:5-25)

One of those scattered by the persecution was Philip. He is mentioned also in 21:8 as "Philip the evangelist." He was not the apostle Philip (all the apostles were still in Jerusalem, Acts 8:1), but was apparently one of the Seven chosen by the Jerusalem church to care for the widows (6:5).

Philip went from Jerusalem to the city of Samaria.[4] Christ

---

[2]See discussion on Acts 6:1,2.

[3]See discussion on 7:54-60.

[4]This was the OT name. Herod the Great had rebuilt Samaria and it was ordinarily called Sebaste in NT times. If the article be omitted from "city"

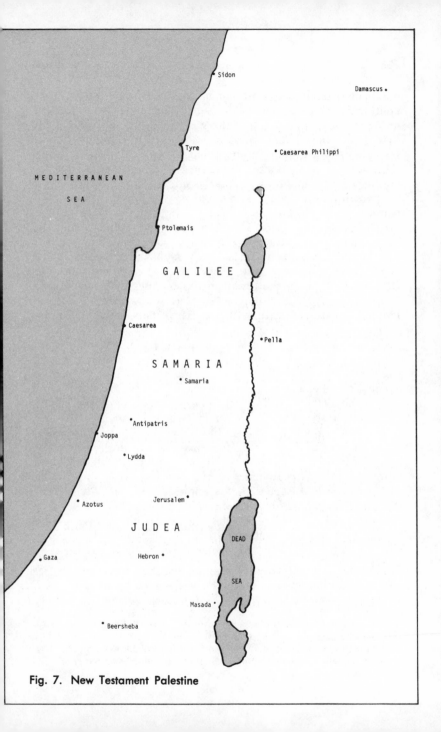

Fig. 7. New Testament Palestine

had once spent two days at Sychar, just seven miles away (John
4:40). Philip's preaching to the Samaritans indicated a growing
awareness in the church that the gospel was intended for others
than Jews only. The Samaritans were greatly despised by the
Jews because of their impure blood lines and their religious
deviations from orthodox Judaism. Following the fall of the
northern kingdom in 722 B.C., the largely depopulated region
was resettled by colonists brought in by the Assyrians from
various parts of their empire (II Kings 17:24). They inter-
married with the Jews who had been left behind, and the
"Samaritans" were their descendants. The rebuilding of the
temple and the walls at Jerusalem brought opposition from the
Samaritans, and eventually a rival temple was built on Mt.
Gerizim. Ever since, the Jews had "no dealings with the Samaritans" (John 4:9), and the feeling was reciprocated. Thus for
Philip to share his faith with the Samaritans was a most un-
common act.

Philip's preaching was accompanied by numerous supernatural signs as tokens that God's power was behind the new
movement. As a result many of the Samaritans believed Philip
as he announced the good news of Jesus Christ, and they
demonstrated their faith by receiving Christian baptism. Among
those who responded was a sorcerer named Simon,[5] who previously had gained a considerable following through his mystical pretensions. Such religious charlatans were a frequent
occurrence in the ancient world; one had ingratiated himself
into the court of the Roman proconsul on Cyprus (13:8). Simon
was particularly attracted by the miracles, and this may explain
the superficiality of his faith (8:13).

Reports reached the apostles at Jerusalem regarding the
Samaritans' response to the gospel, and they immediately dispatched Peter and John[6] to Samaria. Upon their arrival, they

(as in manuscripts D and E), then "a city of Samaria" could indicate some
other place, such as Gitta, noted by Justin Martyr as the birthplace of Simon
Magus (*First Apology*, Ch. 26). The article is included, however, in Aleph,
A, and B.

[5]He is commonly called Simon Magus in Christian history. The word
"Magus" is derived from the Greek word for sorcerer (*magos*).

[6]This is John's last appearance in Acts. He is referred to, however, in 12:2,
and was present in Jerusalem during one of Paul's visits (Gal. 2:9).

prayed for the Samaritans that they might receive the Holy Spirit. Although they did not receive the Holy Spirit until the apostles came from Jerusalem, the account indicates that the Samaritans had genuinely believed and were saved. The words used of them, "believed Philip," "received the word of God," and "were baptized," suggest nothing lacking in their faith or obedience. Apparently Philip recognized no lack for he baptized them. Even Peter and John did not question their faith, for they preached nothing further to them. Hence it must not have been the regenerating work of the Holy Spirit which was lacking, but the external manifestations which accompanied the Spirit's arrival at Pentecost. This was the period of transition from the OT dispensation to the NT era, and these believers at Samaria were in a position similar to the believers at Jerusalem prior to Pentecost.

Why was the Spirit withheld until Peter and John arrived? Ritualists insist that an apostolic laying on of hands was required. Yet Saul of Tarsus received the Spirit through the imposition of the hands of Ananias, who was not an apostle (9:17). Others use this passage to show that reception of the Spirit is an event entirely separate from regeneration (a "second blessing"), and hold that a person can be born again but not necessarily possess the Holy Spirit, ignoring such passages as Romans 8:9.

The answer to this problem must not ignore the social and historical situation. The Samaritans needed to be shown the truth that "salvation is of the Jews" (John 4:22). The schism which had plagued the Jews and Samaritans would doubtless have been carried over into the church, unless some method should be devised to preserve the unity of the church. There could very easily have been Jewish Christians who would have "no dealings with" Samaritan Christians (cf. John 4:9). By withholding the Spirit's coming until the apostles arrived, God insured that the work of Philip was united with that of the Jerusalem apostles. Peter used the keys committed to him (Matt. 16:18, 19) to open the door officially to the Samaritans, just as he did to 3,000 Jews at Pentecost, and would again a little later to the gentiles at the house of Cornelius (chap. 10). It would be a great mistake, however, to treat this incident at

Samaria as normative for all subsequent believers. A look at
the Spirit's coming upon Saul (9:17) and Cornelius (10:44)
will reveal considerable differences, so that the Samaritan
experience was not the regular pattern in the Book of Acts.

Simon Magus incurred the denunciation of Peter because he
sought to purchase from the apostles the authority to bestow
the Holy Spirit.[7] It is apparent that the bestowal of the Spirit
was accompanied by sufficient supernatural phenomena to
make it most attractive to a person like Simon. The nature of
Peter's rebuke makes the spiritual status of Simon highly questionable. In all likelihood his belief (8:13) was only super-
ficial and not true saving faith, as the following reasons indicate.
(1) His belief seems to have been based upon the miracles
which he beheld (vs. 13), and could be mere intellectual assent.
Jesus usually discounted that kind of faith (John 2:23-25; 6:26,
66). It is true that the same word is used for "believe" of Simon
and the rest of the Samaritans, but the context must indicate
the content of the belief. (2) Simon is contrasted to the others
throughout the account. (3) The particular type of rebuke given
to Simon makes it doubtful that he was saved. "Thy silver be
with thee into perdition" (literal translation). "Thou hast neither part nor lot in this matter." "Thy heart is not right." The
expression "gall of bitterness and bond of iniquity" was OT
terminology descriptive of most serious offenses (Deut. 29:18,
20). (4) Simon exhibited no personal sense of sin, but only a
fear of judgment. (5) The consistent testimony of church tradition associates Simon Magus with heresy. Justin Martyr, who
lived about 100 years later in Samaria, said Simon became a
Gnostic.

C. *The Conversion of the Ethiopian Eunuch* (8:26-40)

When the apostles returned to Jerusalem, Philip may have
gone with them. The instructions for him to go on the road
from Jerusalem to Gaza suggest this. He was informed by an
angel of the Lord[8] to make his journey to the vicinity of Gaza,

---

[7]His action has given to the vocabulary of church history the word
"simony," which denotes the buying and selling of ecclesiastical rights and
offices.

[8]Greek: *angelos de kuriou* (no article, hence not "the angel of the Lord").

the ancient Philistine city south and west of Jerusalem near the Mediterranean coast. Old Testament Gaza had been destroyed in 93 B.C., and the city had been rebuilt on a site nearby in 57 B.C. The angel's mention of "desert" referred either to the site of the older deserted city or else to the road itself which proceeds through desolate country.

Traveling the same road was an Ethiopian eunuch who occupied a position of great responsibility, having oversight of the queen's treasury. Candace was the dynastic title used by a number of women rulers in Ethiopia (corresponding to modern Nubia).[9] This use would be similar to the titles "Pharaoh" and "Caesar" in Egypt and Rome. The term "eunuch" was used in two senses. In Matthew 19:12 it is used of physically castrated men, or of those who are born without sexual capacity. Such persons often served as harem keepers in the ancient world and some rose to high government positions. In the LXX (Greek version of the OT), however, the term *eunouchos* was used of Potiphar who was married (Gen. 39:1), and hence the sense of "court officer" must be intended, without the additional idea of physical impairment. One cannot, therefore, be certain whether or not the Ethiopian was a physical eunuch.

The eunuch was evidently a proselyte to the Jewish religion, inasmuch as he had just been to Jerusalem to engage in worship. If he were physically mutilated, he could not have been a full proselyte (i.e., "a proselyte of righteousness," to use the Jewish term), for such were prohibited complete access to the sanctuary (Deut. 23:1). He must then have been a "proselyte of the gate," one whose adherence to Judaism was only partial.

Both Philip and the eunuch were prepared for the interview. Philip had the direct command of God. The eunuch had been meditating upon Isaiah 53:7, 8. Being prompted by the Spirit[10] to intercept the eunuch, Philip used the remarkable prophecy regarding the Suffering Servant to show how the reference was

---

[9]F. F. Bruce, however, cites support for understanding the title as denoting the queen-mother, *The Book of Acts,* p. 186, ftn.

[10]Whether the same divine messenger addressed Philip throughout is uncertain. The speaker is called "an angel of the Lord" in verse 26 and "the Spirit" in verse 29. If only one speaker is involved, then the second reference apparently refers to the angel as a spirit being. If separate speakers are meant, the second is most probably the Holy Spirit.

to Jesus, whose suffering and death had accomplished exactly what Isaiah had predicted. Philip's explanations must have been sufficiently broad to include the necessity of a personal response and the need for Christian baptism. When the eunuch saw a nearby pool, he requested baptism at the hands of Philip. Although the ordinary Jew might well have regarded the eunuch as unqualified — he was a eunuch, and in all probability he was also a gentile — Philip had caught the spirit of the Great Commission, and promptly baptized him. (Verse 37 has scant textual support and is omitted by most recent versions.[11] Doubtless something like what it states did occur, but Luke apparently did not write it.)

After the interview and the baptism, the Spirit of the Lord "caught away" Philip. He next appeared at Azotus (OT Ashdod), twenty miles north of Gaza. One should not read miracles into the text that are not clearly there. Nevertheless, the expression "caught away"[12] seems too strong to describe a natural departure, and may denote a miraculous removal, as in the OT instances of Ezekiel (Ezek. 3:12, 14; 8:3) and Elijah (I Kings 18:12; II Kings 2:16). Philip then made his way up the coast to Caesarea. He must have settled there, for he next appears in the record at Caesarea more than twenty years later with a house and four daughters (21:8, 9).

II. THE CONVERSION OF SAUL (9:1-31)

A. *Saul's Vision on the Road* (9:1-9)

As the persecution described in 8:1-4 proceeded, Saul expanded his efforts beyond Jerusalem itself. Going to the high priest,[13] Saul secured official credentials authorizing him to extradite any Christians whom he might find in Damascus. Apparently his quarry were ones who had fled Jerusalem and sought sanctuary in Damascus. Roman practice allowed the Jewish Sanhedrin to control Jewish affairs even outside Palestine

---

[11]The verse does not appear in our most ancient authorities: P45 P74 Aleph A B C P. Consequently, it is omitted by ASV, RSV, NEB, and NASB.

[12]Greek: *hērpasen.*

[13]If this was prior to A.D. 36 as seems probable, the high priest was Caiaphas.

proper. Synagogue rulers at Damascus could therefore be expected to cooperate with anyone who bore such authorization from Jerusalem.

The believers being sought by Saul are called those of "the Way." This is the first of numerous instances in Acts where this designation is employed.[14]

As Saul and his companions neared the end of their long journey,[15] a blinding light from heaven felled him, and a voice from heaven addressed him. It is clear from other Scripture that he also saw Jesus at this time (9:17, 27; 22:14; 26:16; I Cor. 9:1; 15:8). His companions saw nothing but the light (22:9), and understood nothing of the conversation. Saul, however, saw the risen Christ, and responded with the words, "Who art thou, Lord?" It may be questioned whether *kurie* should be translated "Lord" (remember Saul did not yet know the identity of the Speaker) or merely as the respectful "sir." It seems improbable, at least to this writer, that the rabbinically-trained Saul would have meant a simple "sir" in the presence of an obvious divine manifestation of some sort. Hence his question should be understood as a request for this divine personage to identify himself. When this Lord of glory identified himself as Jesus, Saul's persecuting hatred was turned to faith, for he had been confronted with the basic concepts needed for salvation. He later wrote: "If thou shalt confess with thy mouth Jesus as Lord, and shall believe in thy heart that God raised him from the dead, thou shalt be saved" (Rom. 10:9 ASV). (The last part of 9:5, "it is hard for thee to kick against the pricks," should be omitted here on textual grounds. It was probably added in some manuscripts from 26:14 where it properly belongs.)

B. *Saul's Commission in Damascus* (9:10-25)

Saul was taken into Damascus and lodged in the house of Judas on Straight Street, which still runs through Damascus. Meanwhile, the Lord appeared to Ananias, who was neither an apostle nor a deacon but an ordinary Christian, and directed him to restore Saul's eyesight and deliver to him a commission. The

---

[14]Other occurrences are: 19:9, 23; 22:4; 24:14, 22.

[15]Damascus was approximately 150 miles from Jerusalem, and required from 6 to 8 days of normal travel.

choice of Ananias for this task made it clear that Saul of Tarsus was not dependent upon the Twelve, and also that an apostle was not required for bestowing the Spirit (as might have been concluded from the case in Samaria). Inasmuch as Ananias was not an official, and merely acted as God's spokesman, no one ever accused Paul of being dependent upon Ananias for his apostolic authority (see the argument of Gal. 1).

Saul's commission designated him as Christ's chosen vessel to accomplish a remarkable ministry. He would be the instrument whereby the name of Christ would be carried far and wide

Fig. 8. The Wall of Damascus. The abutment at the left of the photograph is identified by some as the probable place where Paul was lowered through a window to escape the plot on his life. Levant Photo Service

to gentiles, Israelites, and even kings. At the same time he would not be immune from misfortune, for suffering would be a significant feature of his career. Doubtless it was due in no small part to this advance warning that the sufferings he later incurred did not discourage him but rather confirmed his calling.

By the imposition of Ananias' hands, Saul was filled with the Holy Spirit. He also received his eyesight, submitted to Christian baptism, and then partook of food after his three days of fasting. Inasmuch as the filling of the Holy Spirit is mentioned here, it should probably be inferred that Saul's regeneration had occurred previously on the Damascus Road (and at that time he had experienced the baptism of the Spirit which made him a part of the body of Christ).

Saul preached his new faith in the synagogues of Damascus, but eventually the unconverted Jews plotted to slay him. In 9:25 the original text reads "his disciples." Saul's preaching had already won some adherents in Damascus, and they lowered him at night through a window in the city wall by means of a large basket so that he might escape those who were watching the gates. According to II Corinthians 11:32, 33, the Jews had enlisted the aid of the governor under the Nabatean king, Aretas, to apprehend Paul. Although Damascus was not a Nabatean city, it is supposed by some that a colony of Nabateans lived in Damascus and were governed by an ethnarch appointed by Aretas IV, and it was these who made the plot.[16] D. J. Wiseman, however, explains that by the time of Saul's conversion, Damascus itself was actually governed by an ethnarch appointed by Aretas, who had defeated his son-in-law Herod Antipas.[17]

C. Saul's Reception in Jerusalem (9:26-31)

When Saul returned to Jerusalem he found no immediate welcome. His former associates, of course, would have hated him. When he tried to join the Christians, his reputation as a persecutor was well remembered, and a strategem for further assaults was suspected. Barnabas, however, demonstrated the appropriateness of his name "son of encouragement" (4:36), and in-

[16]So F. F. Bruce, *The Book of the Acts*, p. 204.
[17]"Damascus," *The New Bible Dictionary* (Grand Rapids, 1962), p. 289.

troduced Saul to the group.[18] His introduction indicated that
Saul was a most extraordinary convert — one who actually had
the qualifications of an apostle, for he had seen the resurrected
Christ, had been commissioned by him, and had been preaching
boldly in Damascus.[19]

After the fears of the Jerusalem Christians were removed, Saul
engaged in a preaching ministry with particular concentration
upon reaching Hellenists.[20] This was the very work in which
Stephen had engaged before his death. What must have been
Saul's feelings as he took up the same task which once he had
helped to interrupt? It was not long,[21] however, before the
Hellenist Jews laid plans to kill him. Additional information is
given in 22:17-21, where by a trance in the temple God warned
him of this opposition and ordered him to leave Jerusalem. His
Christian friends then conducted him to Caesarea where he
doubtless took a ship for his trip to Tarsus in Cilicia. Mention
of these Christian "brethren" (vs. 39) indicates either that new
converts had been made in Jerusalem since the scattering of
8:1, or else that many had returned to the city.

Verse 31 is Luke's summary, showing that in spite of the se-
verity of the persecution he has described, "rest" for the churches
finally came when the chief persecutor was converted. This
statement contains the only mention in Acts of the presence of
Christians in Galilee. Although many suggestions have been
offered to account for this circumstance, Munck's explanation
is the most likely. He avers that the progress of the gospel in
Galilee faced no special problems, and that from the historian's
viewpoint, the most significant events for future development
occurred elsewhere.[22]

[18]The mention of "apostles" in 9:27 must be a generalizing plural, inasmuch as the only apostle met by Saul at this time was Peter unless James the
Lord's brother be considered an apostle in the wider sense (Gal. 1:18, 19).

[19]It has been suggested that Barnabas and Saul may have been previously
acquainted inasmuch as their homes in Cyprus and Cilicia were near each
other. No positive evidence exists, however, and the information possessed by
Barnabas may have come from Paul himself or others from Damascus.

[20]KJV: "Grecians"; Greek: *Hellēnistas*.

[21]Galatians 1:18 indicates that his total time in Jerusalem was only 15 days.

[22]Johannes Munck, *The Acts of the Apostles* in The Anchor Bible series
(Garden City, 1967), p. 88.

III. THE CONTINUED MINISTRY OF PETER (9:32-43)

A. *The Healing of Aenaeus at Lydda* (9:32-35)

The author now picks up the story of Peter, for it was vitally important to show how the church came to accept uncircumcised gentiles as true Christians before Paul's missionary journeys could be properly understood.

It all began with a preaching tour undertaken by Peter. When he came to Lydda (modern Lod, site of Israel's leading jet airport) he met some believers. Perhaps Philip had preached there earlier as he had journeyed northward (8:40). Peter met Aenaeus, who had been bedfast for eight years with a condition of paralysis. Whether he was a Christian when Peter met him is uncertain, although his being termed "a certain man" (i.e., not "disciple" or "believer") might suggest that he was not (contra. the description of Dorcas as a "disciple" in 9:36). Peter's words, "Jesus Christ heals you," made it clear that Christ was still working among men (1:1), although now it was through the instrumentality of Spirit-filled men. The instruction to "make your bed"[23] could possibly be rendered "prepare a table for yourself." Whichever was meant, the man was powerless to respond without a miracle. As a result of the healing there was a favorable response to the gospel throughout Lydda and the whole vicinity of the plain of Sharon.

B. *The Raising of Dorcas at Joppa* (9:36-43)

Dorcas (her Hebrew name was Tabitha) was a female disciple at Joppa who was noted for her practical Christianity. She devoted her talents as a seamstress to the benefit of others, particularly to needy widows. When she died, the believers sent for Peter, knowing that he was in the vicinity. (Joppa was on the Mediterranean coast, ten miles from Lydda. It is today called Jaffa, and is adjacent to the modern city of Tel Aviv.) They did not ask for her to be raised, although the delay in burial may indicate what was in their minds. Peter put everyone outside the room, much in the manner of Jesus at the home of Jairus

---

[23]Greek: *strōson seautōi,* literally "spread for yourself." The object of "spread" must be inferred.

(to which raising Peter had been one of three witnesses, Mark 5:35-43). He may not have known God's will in the matter at first, so he prayed, and we must conclude that the subsequent raising was an answer to prayer.

At Joppa Peter lodged with Simon, a tanner. Jews felt an abhorrence for members of the tanning trades. Such workmen handled skins from ceremonially unclean animals, and were thus regarded as Levitically impure. Tanners usually resided outside of town to be near sufficient water and also because their operations were so malodorous.[24] Peter's disregard of Jewish scruples in this instance may indicate his broadening outlook, and is an interesting preface to the events of Acts 10.

QUESTIONS FOR DISCUSSION

1. What were some of the beneficial results of persecution?
2. Why was the Holy Spirit withheld from the Samaritans until Peter and John arrived?
3. Do you think Simon Magus was a genuine believer?
4. Does Ananias' commissioning of Saul invalidate the argument of Galatians 1:1 that Saul's authority was not of men nor by man?
5. Did Saul become a saved man on the Damascus Road, or when Ananias laid hands on him?

---

[24]See D. J. Wiseman, "Arts and Crafts," *The New Bible Dictionary,* p. 92.

Chapter 6

TO CAESAREA AND ANTIOCH
(Acts 10-12)

The importance of Cornelius to the history of the Christian movement is indicated by the space devoted to this episode in Acts. It is set forth in great detail in Acts 10, and then reiterated at some length in Acts 11. The issue that it posed was crucial for future progress. The gospel had been well established in Jerusalem and was being extended throughout the rest of Palestine. It was only a matter of time, however, until the borders of the Jewish community would be reached. and the problem of gentile eligibility would be raised. It may well be that the question had already been faced to a limited degree. The Ethiopian eunuch may have been a gentile (Acts 8). Some of the preaching among Greeks at Antioch may have already begun (Acts 11:19, 20). The age-old cleavage between Jew and gentile must certainly have caused these contacts to be viewed with grave suspicion in certain quarters. What was needed was a test case to deal squarely with the issue. Vitally important was the necessity of knowing exactly what God's will was in the matter. The episode with Cornelius provided the occasion for the young church to confront the matter which it could not much longer sidestep. The implications of what took place have affected the character of the church from that time on.

I. THE CONVERSION OF CORNELIUS (10:1–11:18)

A. *The Vision of Cornelius* (10:1-8)

In the city of Caesarea there was stationed a military man named Cornelius. Caesarea was the residence of the Roman procurator of Judea and was the capital of the province. Cornelius was a centurion in the Roman army, attached to the cohort[1] known as the Italian cohort, probably because its original composition was of men from Italy.

[1]Each Roman legion at full strength consisted of ten cohorts (Greek: *speira,*

Fig. 9. Modern Tel Aviv, adjacent to the ancient city of Joppa where Peter stayed by the shore with Simon a tanner. Photo by the author

When Luke calls Cornelius a man who "feared God,"[2] he was using an expression which when applied to gentiles in the NT meant that they were adherents to Judaism to a limited extent (i.e., "proselytes of the gate"). They attended synagogue worship, acknowledged the God of Israel, and complied with some Jewish customs. They were not circumcised, however, and thus were regarded by Jews as not full "proselytes of righteousness."

As Cornelius was observing one of the regular Jewish times for prayer,[3] he saw in a vision an angel of God who told him that his prayers had not been fruitless. Although Cornelius had come a long way from paganism, he still was unsaved at this time (see 11:14). He had followed much of the light he had,

translated as "band" in KJV) of approximately 600 men each. Each cohort contained six centuries under the command of a centurion. Cornelius thus had authority over 100 men in the Italian cohort.

[2]Greek: *phoboumenos ton theon.* A similar expression is *sebomenos ton theon* (used in 16:14, *et al.*).

[3]The ninth hour by Jewish reckoning was the equivalent of 3 p.m.

but he had not gone as far as he could have even in Judaism, for he had stopped short of following OT instruction as to becoming a full proselyte through circumcision. Nevertheless, God by his angel sent him more light and he responded. He was instructed to send for Simon Peter, who was staying with Simon a tanner at Joppa. The house could be found by the shore, for tanners used considerable water in their occupation.

Immediately Cornelius dispatched to Joppa two of his servants and a soldier who apparently shared his superior's interest in Jewish religion. Inasmuch as it was already past 3 p.m., they may not have left until the next morning. If they left on the day of the vision, they must have traveled much of the night to cover thirty miles by noon of the next day.

B. *The Vision of Peter* (10:9-23)

God not only supernaturally directed Cornelius but Peter as well. Peter was a Jew with all the normal prejudices of his people. Though he was now a Christian, his normal aversions did not disappear overnight. The early Christians did not immediately begin preaching to gentiles. It took the divine intervention recorded in this chapter to bring it about.

At noon on the day after the messengers from Cornelius set out on their mission, Peter went up to the roof of Simon's house to pray. The flat rooftops of Palestinian homes were often used for relaxation. Simon's rooftop may have been protected by an awning inasmuch as it was being utilized at noon. While Peter waited for his meal to be prepared, he fell into a trance and saw a sheet-like vessel lowered from heaven containing both clean and unclean animals. He heard the voice of the Lord (Jesus?) telling him to kill and eat. When Peter remonstrated that he had always observed Levitical distinctions, he was told, "What God hath cleansed, that call not thou common" (vs. 15).

Peter was perplexed about the meaning of the vision. On the surface it seemed to mean that the Mosaic laws of ritual cleanness were no longer to be observed. But was this all that was implied? God provided the answer as the three gentiles from Cornelius came to ask for Peter. By instructing Peter to go with them, the Holy Spirit enabled Peter to draw his own conclusion about these gentiles. Peter stated his understanding

Fig. 10. A Village of Flat-roofed Houses (Dhana in ancient Edom). The stairs can be seen outside the house in the center of the picture. On such a housetop Peter was praying when he saw the vision of the sheet. Levant Photo Service

later to Cornelius: "God hath showed me that I should not call any man common or unclean" (vs. 28). If the food laws of the Jews no longer were valid, there was no real reason to avoid social contact with gentiles, for those distinctions lay at the heart of Jewish clannishness. Therefore, he lodged these gentiles overnight, and set out with them the next day for Caesarea, accompanied by six Christian Jews from Joppa (11:12).

C. *The Preaching of Peter* (10:24-43)

When Peter approached the quarters of Cornelius, his host fell reverently at his feet, mindful of the fact that Peter was the one whom the angel had directed him to summon. The apostle refused any such honors, however well meant, and went with Cornelius into the house to meet the assembled friends and family of the centurion.

For Peter, the Jew, to enter a gentile dwelling was a distinct breach of custom. Even though he was now a Christian, he made it clear that he would never have violated his Jewish practices without a vision from God. Happily, Peter was not so enslaved to his traditions that he was insensitive to further light. When Cornelius explained that he too had received a divine message, it was obvious that God had brought both parties together.

Peter began his message by noting that God does not show partiality to Jews above gentiles (vs. 34). "Respecter of persons" (KJV) or "one to show partiality" (NASB) means literally "face taker."[4] He meant that God does not save men on the basis of their individual appearance or race. The same thought occurs in the OT: Deuteronomy 10:17; II Chronicles 19:7; Job 34:19. Peter was learning the meaning of Jesus' words, "Other sheep I have which are not of this fold; them also I must bring" (John 10:16).

Verse 35 must not be understood as teaching salvation by works, for "accepted with him"[5] is not equivalent to "saved" inasmuch as the angel had told Cornelius that he still needed to be saved (11:14). Peter meant that God was obviously not interested in Jews only; for it was clear that in the case of

---

[4]Greek: *prosōpolēmptēs*.
[5]Greek: *dektos autōi*.

Cornelius, a gentile who had become a God-fearer and had performed appropriate acts of righteousness, God was desirous that he be offered the gospel of salvation just as the Jews. The eligibility of Cornelius as a candidate to receive the gospel was as valid as that of any Jew.

Peter's explanation of the gospel presupposed that his audience had some familiarity with the career of Jesus. "Ye know" (vs. 37), he said, but nevertheless he proceeded at least in outline to rehearse the general movement of Christ's ministry. Beginning with John's baptism he sketched Christ's career in Galilee, Judea, and Jerusalem. He mentioned his activities of healing and other good deeds, and then spoke of his crucifixion, resurrection, and post-resurrection appearances. Jesus, he said, was the one predicted by the prophets who would provide forgiveness of sins to those who would believe, and he had commanded Peter and the other eyewitnesses to proclaim this message to men. This simple outline is similar to the arrangement of material in the Gospel of Mark, and is perhaps the clearest NT example of the *kerygma*, the earliest form in which the apostolic proclamation of the gospel was apparently couched.

D. *The Descent of the Holy Spirit* (10:44-48)

It was while Peter was still speaking that the Holy Spirit came upon the hearers. In comparison with the other instances in Acts where the coming of the Holy Spirit is described (Acts 2:1-4; 8:15-17; 9:17; 19:1-6), certain differences will be noted. The Spirit's coming was not dependent upon public confession or an interval of time after accepting Christ. The Holy Spirit was not prayed for. His coming did not follow water baptism nor the laying on of anyone's hands. He came upon these gentiles as they listened with receptive hearts to the message of Peter. When he spoke of forgiveness of sins as being available to those who believe in Christ (vs. 43), their immediate response must have been to believe, and on that basis the Holy Spirit came. This agrees with what Peter himself later intimated in reporting the incident to Jerusalem: "God therefore gave to them the same gift as He gave to us also after believing in the Lord Jesus" (11:17, NASB). Paul wrote, "Received ye the Spirit by the works of the law, or by the hearing of faith?" (Gal. 3:2)

The Holy Spirit is thus God's provision to men when they truly believe in Christ. Faith is the common denominator in all of the instances described in Acts, and any differences should be considered in the light of historical factors that existed.[6]

"The gift of the Holy Spirit" means "the gift which is the Holy Spirit."[7] This experience was the gentile counterpart of Pentecost, as 11:17 clearly shows, and included both the baptism of the Spirit and the filling of the Spirit. The phenomenon of speaking in tongues was an evidence of the latter (as in 2:4), whether it took the form of foreign languages as at Pentecost (the household and military friends of Cornelius could have included persons from various places in the empire), or was of the variety known at Corinth which required a human interpreter is not certain. The former is perhaps more likely, inasmuch as no interpreters are indicated, and the similarity to Pentecost is especially noted (11:17).

The Jewish Christians who had accompanied Peter were witnesses to these events, and could provide firm support at Jerusalem when Peter was questioned about this matter. Peter himself ordered that Christian baptism be administered to these gentile believers (although he apparently did not perform it himself). This baptism did not bring salvation or the Holy Spirit, but was an act of obedience to Christ's commission, and was the outward testimony to the spiritual realities which had been experienced.

E. *The Explanation to the Jerusalem Church* (11:1-18)

Inasmuch as Peter remained some days in Caesarea, news of the events in Cornelius' household reached Jerusalem before Peter returned. The idea of gentiles being baptized and accepted as part of the church was new to them. Even the Samaritans had some Jewish heritage, and the eunuch (assuming that he was a gentile) had gone home to Ethiopia and posed no delicate problems for the Jerusalem church. Cornelius, however, lived in Palestine, and the practical issues of social relationships would immediately arise.

---

[6]For example, see the discussion on 8:5-25.

[7]Greek: *hē dōrea tou pneumatos tou hagiou.* The genitive here denotes apposition.

By the time of Peter's arrival, trouble was already brewing. "Those of the circumcision"[8] probably means not just "those who were circumcised" (NASB), for all the Jerusalem Christians were circumcised, but those who were strongly insistent upon such Mosaic traditions. They would have been the most tradition-minded of the Hebrews, as contrasted with the Hellenists.[9] The word "contended" in verse 2 comes from a root which means "to judge between" or "make a distinction."[10] Some of those at Jerusalem were prepared to argue over the distinctions that they felt must be maintained between Jew and gentile. The specific charge made against Peter was that he had entered a gentile dwelling and had eaten with those uncircumcised folk. This, of course, was not unrelated to the problem in 15:1, 5, but merely put the emphasis at a different place.

These verses give an insight into the functioning of the early church. The members at Jerusalem had no hesitancy about challenging Peter, and he in turn did not issue any authoritative fiat to squelch them. The congregation functioned quite democratically in this confrontation.

Peter explained the facts which had occurred. Luke obviously regarded this experience with Cornelius as a pivotal point in the history of the church, inasmuch as he repeats much of the material from the previous chapter. By rehearsing the incident with considerable detail, Peter made it clear that this extension of the gospel to the gentiles was not some idea of his own to enlarge the church, but was God's doing from beginning to end. God had provided a vision for Peter, he had sent an angel to Cornelius, and he had sent the Holy Spirit upon the gentiles in the same fashion as upon Jewish believers at Pentecost. It was not a matter of questionable tactics on the part of the apostle. It was God's own action.

The result was that the opponents ceased their opposition[11]

---

[8]Greek: *hoi ek peritomēs.*

[9]See discussion on 6:1.

[10]Greek: *diekrinonto*, from *diakrinō*. The middle is used here and 10:20, and the active occurs in 11:12. The middle is commonly given the sense of "doubt" or "contend," and the meaning of "make a distinction" is reserved for the active. However, in this narrative the root idea may be present to some extent in all the occurrences.

[11]Greek: *hēsuchasan*, "they kept silent, quieted down."

and glorified God for this clear demonstration of his will in salvation. The subject is the same for the two verbs "kept silent" and "glorified God," so that we cannot assume a grudging acquiescence. The same persons also praised God for saving gentiles. The fact that some in this church later raised the problem again is not too surprising, since even Peter acted inconsistently on a subsequent occasion (Gal. 2:11-14). With the vindication of gentile evangelization now a matter of record at Jerusalem, the church there was prepared to cooperate in the new activity at Antioch.

II. THE FOUNDING OF THE CHURCH AT ANTIOCH (11:19-30)

A. *The Founders at Antioch* (11:19-21)

This passage takes the reader back in time to the events of Acts 8:1, 4, and describes what was occurring in the north at the same time that the happenings in Samaria, Caesarea, and that general region were taking place. The persecution brought on by the affair of Stephen drove some of the Christians to Phoenicia (whose major cities were Tyre and Sidon), Cyprus, and Antioch. The initial preaching was confined to the Jewish communities. Soon, however, some Cypriot and Cyrenian Jewish Christians began to proclaim the gospel to Greeks in Antioch. Their efforts were mightily blessed by the Lord, and many converts were made.

Antioch was the third largest city in the Roman Empire at this time (after Rome and Alexandria).[12] It had a large Jewish colony, and many proselytes had attached themselves to Judaism in Antioch.[13] One of them has already been mentioned in Acts.[14] The city knew great moral degradation, for the temple of Daphne with its ritual prostitution was only five miles away and exerted its influence in Antioch.

The manuscripts vary at verse 20, some containing the term "Greeks" (i.e., gentiles) and others "Hellenists" (i.e., Greek-

---

[12]Josephus *The Jewish War* III.2.4.
[13]*Ibid.*, VII.3.3.
[14]Nicolas (Acts 6:5).

cultured Jews).[15] The former term[16] is found in manuscripts
A, D, a corrector of Aleph, and P[74], and the sense is certainly
favored by the context which distinguishes them from the "Jews
only" of verse 19. If the reference were merely to Greek-cultured
Jews, there was no particular reason to mention the fact for
people of this sort had been evangelized beginning at Pentecost.
The alternate reading "Hellenists"[17] also has good manuscript
support, but if it be adopted, the sense must be "Greek speakers"
and must include gentiles as well as Jews. The second century
Anti-Marcionite Prologue to Luke states that Luke was an
Antiochian of Syria,[18] and this is confirmed by Eusebius in the
fourth century.[19]

B. *The Leaders at Antioch* (11:22-26)

Just as the Jerusalem church sent Peter and John to visit the
work in Samaria, it sent Barnabas to investigate the situation
in Antioch. If this occurred subsequent to the episode of Cornelius, then the vindication of gentile evangelization had already
occurred, and Barnabas could encourage the new enterprise.
Barnabas himself was a Cypriot Jew (4:36), although not one
of the original evangelizers at Antioch (11:20). His character as
a good man, full of the Spirit, and possessed of vision ("faith")
for the work, made him a happy choice for the task.

As Barnabas saw the rapid growth of the church at Antioch,
he recognized its need for more leadership. He was the one who
had introduced Saul to the church at Jerusalem (9:27), and
realized that Saul with his great gift of teaching could be of
much use in this city where Jewish feelings would not be
running as high as in Jerusalem. Saul had been in Tarsus from
seven to ten years, having been sent there by the Jerusalem

---

[15]The KJV term "Grecians" is somewhat ambiguous, and does not indicate
precisely who these people were.

[16]Greek: *Hellēnas.*

[17]Greek: *Hellēnistas,* found in B, E, and the Byzantine text.

[18]A translation of the text is given by T. W. Manson, *Studies in the Gospels
and Epistles,* ed. Matthew Black (Philadelphia, 1962), p. 49.

[19]Eusebius, *Ecclesiastical History* (III.4), trans. Roy J. Deferrari (Washington, reprinted 1969), p. 142.

church (9:30). Barnabas made a search[20] for him, and then brought him to Antioch where both men engaged for an entire year in a teaching ministry.

It was at Antioch that the name "Christians" was first applied to the believers. In all likelihood the name was first coined by outsiders, inasmuch as the church called itself "brethren," "disciples," "those of the Way," or "those who were believing." It is not probable that Jews bestowed the name, for they would not use the name of their Messiah (Greek: *Christos*) to denote those whom they regarded as heretics. In the other two NT occurrences of the term, once it is used by Agrippa II (26:28), and once it is used by Peter to report the language of persecutors (I Peter 4:16). The verb "were called" means "to bear the name,"[21] and can suggest a bestowal from without. The name consists of the title "Christ" with the suffix "-ian" denoting an adherent.[22]

C. *The Ministry at Antioch* (11:27-30)

There was continued close cooperation between the Jerusalem and Antioch churches, and prophets from Jerusalem ministered in the new work along with Barnabas and Saul. This is the first mention of NT prophets, whose function apparently included prediction as well as proclamation of the word of God. Agabus who prophesied the famine appears again in 21:10.

The famine which Agabus predicted occurred during the reign of the Roman emperor Claudius (A.D. 41-54). Although history has not yet confirmed the fact of a worldwide famine at that time, there are records of frequent famines during this period. Suetonius recorded the following:

> Once, after a series of droughts had caused a scarcity of grain, a mob stopped Claudius in the Forum and pelted him so hard with curses and stale crusts that he had difficulty in regaining the Palace by a side-door; as a result he took all possible steps to import corn, even during the winter — insuring merchants against the loss of their ships in stormy weather (which guaranteed them a good return on their ventures), and

---

[20]The verb *anazētēsai* and the special mention of finding Saul suggest that some difficulty was involved in locating him.

[21]Greek: *chrēmatisai*.

[22]As in the case of the name "Herodians" to denote supporters of Herod (Matt. 22:16; Mark 3:6; 12:13).

offering a bounty for every new grain-transport built, proportionate to its tonnage.[23]

Josephus reports a great famine in Judea during the procuratorships of Cuspius Fadus (A.D. 44-46) and Tiberius Alexander (A.D. 46-48).

> . . . Under these procurators that great famine happened in Judea, in which queen Helena bought corn in Egypt at a great expense, and distributed it to those that were in want, as I have related already.[24]

The Antioch church took prompt steps to alleviate the food shortage among their Jerusalem brethren. Although there is no record of a community of goods in Antioch, the same spirit of unity prevailed among them in their relation to Jerusalem. Barnabas and Saul were delegated to take the gifts to Jerusalem.[25] The gifts were delivered to the elders,[26] who perhaps had taken over some of the duties of the Seven (6:1ff.) since the persecution had necessitated some reorganization.

III. THE HERODIAN PERSECUTION (12:1-25)

The first persecution of the church had been instigated by the temple authorities — the priests and Sadducees (4:1). Later the most popular of the religious parties, the Pharisees, joined in attacking the church under the relentless leadership of Saul of Tarsus (8:1, 3). With the entrance of Herod Agrippa I into active persecution, the political interests of Palestine joined the fray, and opposition to the church was thus practically universal in the land of the Jews. Acts 12 marks the close of a section in Luke's history, and the author will then shift his focus to Antioch and the westward march of the gospel toward Rome.

A. *James Beheaded* (12:1, 2)

The persecutor this time was Herod Agrippa I, a nephew of Herod Antipas (murderer of John the Baptist, and the ruler

---

[23]"Claudius" (XVIII), *The Twelve Caesars,* trans. Robert Graves (London, 1957), p. 192.

[24]*Antiquities of the Jews* XX.5.2. The description of Queen Helena's action is given also in *Antiquities* XX.2.5.

[25]See also Josephus *Antiquities* XXX. 15.3, for the high price charged for food in Jerusalem because of the famine.

[26]This is the first mention of Christian elders in Acts.

who questioned Jesus, Matt. 14:1-12; Luke 23:6-12), and grand-son of Herod the Great (in whose reign Jesus was born, Matt. 2:1). He had been reared at Rome with Caligula, and received his realm in stages. He first was appointed king over the terri-tory once ruled by Philip (Luke 3:1), and then acquired the territory of Antipas. In A.D. 41 Claudius added the region of Judea and Samaria which had been governed by Roman pro-curators. This situation continued until A.D. 44 (see Time Chart I). Thus Agrippa I ruled over the largest realm in Palestine since the days of the illustrious Herod the Great forty-five years before. He maintained his power by cultivating favor among the Jews through his support of Judaism.

Although the apostles escaped the previous persecution (8:1), they were apparently the only objects of attack this time. Per-haps James and Peter were the only apostles presently in Jeru-salem.[27] James the son of Zebedee was executed by the sword, probably by beheading.[28] He was the first of the Twelve to die (excluding Judas Iscariot, of course), and his was the only apostle's death recorded in the NT. James had once said he was able to undergo a baptism of suffering, and Jesus confirmed that it would come to pass (Matt. 20:23).

B. *Peter Imprisoned and Delivered* (12:3-19)

Because the death of James pleased the Jewish leaders, Herod proceeded to arrest Peter with the same purpose in mind. He was not executed immediately, however, because the scrupulous Herod would not pollute the feast week. The Feast of Passover (consisting of one meal and its related ritual on Nisan 15) was followed immediately by the week-long Feast of Unleavened Bread. Sometimes, as here, both celebrations were grouped under the single name Passover.[29] This was Peter's third arrest (4:3; 5:18), and remembrance of his previous deliverance from

[27]When Peter was released, he sent word to James the Lord's brother, but none of the Twelve are mentioned (12:17).

[28]The Talmud lists four kinds of capital punishment as available under Jewish law: stoning, burning, slaying by the sword, and choking. "Tract San-hedrin" (Ch. VII), trans. Michael L. Rodkinson, *The Babylonian Talmud* (Boston, 1918), VIII, 149.

[29]The KJV translation "Easter" in vs. 4 is erroneous. The Greek text says *to pascha,* "the passover."

prison (5:19) may have caused extra precautions to be taken. He was put in the care of four squads of four soldiers each. Usual procedure would call for them to serve three-hour watches, with two soldiers chained to the prisoner and two guarding the door.

The church used its only available weapon — prayer. The praying was fervent[30] and continual,[31] even though the church as a whole was astonished when God answered. Nevertheless the spiritual power which prayer unleashed was more than a match for Herod.

On the night before his scheduled execution, Peter was sleeping under full guard when an angel of the Lord[32] released Peter from his chains, opened the inner prison doors, and instructed Peter to follow. When they came to the great iron gate that led out to the city street, it opened automatically.[33]

After the angel disappeared and Peter realized that he was not dreaming, he went immediately to the house of Mary where he apparently knew he would find a group of believers. He must have been well known there for he was recognized by the servant girl Rhoda from his voice alone. The amusing conversation between Rhoda and the others has all the earmarks of an eyewitness report. "It is his angel" (vs. 15) may reflect a Jewish opinion that each person has a guardian angel who can assume the person's own bodily shape and voice. Perhaps they surmised that he had already been executed, and that his "ghost" had appeared.[34]

Knowing that he had only a short time until his escape would be discovered (three hours at the most), Peter silenced their excited chatter, briefly explained what had happened, and then instructed them to explain the situation to James and the other Christian brethren. Apparently the group at Mary's house was

---

[30]Greek: *ektenōs*, vs. 5.

[31]The imperfect periphrastic form *ēn ginomenē* emphasizes the continuing activity.

[32]Greek: *angelos kuriou.* Not "the angel of the Lord" (KJV).

[33]F. F. Bruce suggests that Peter's imprisonment may have been in the Fortress Antonia, at the northwest corner of the temple area. *The Acts of the Apostles* (Grand Rapids, 1952), p. 246.

[34]However, the Greek word here is *angelos,* not *phantasma* as in Matt. 14:26 and Mark 6:49.

not the only Christian body in Jerusalem, and perhaps not even the main one. Peter may have gone there because it was the closest to his prison. The James mentioned in 12:17 is not the prominent apostle (whose murder was recorded in 12:2) but must have been the Lord's brother who seems to have become the acknowledged leader of the Jerusalem church, especially with the departure of the Twelve from the city (Gal. 1:19; 2:9; 2:12; Acts 15:13; 21:18). Peter then left the city and his whereabouts remain a mystery. It is tempting to suppose that at this time he visited Antioch (Gal. 2:11), although that incident probably occurred later.[35] Peter was back in Jerusalem a few years later at the Jerusalem Conference (15:7).

When Peter's escape was discovered in the morning, Herod had the soldiers examined because it appeared to be an "inside job," and then ordered them "led away."[36] Herod himself returned to his capital at Caesarea.[37] He must have been somewhat embarrassed at his inability to come through with his prisoner after raising Jewish hopes over the prospect of Peter's death.

C. Herod Smitten by God (12:20-25)

Herod's death in A.D. 44 is attributed to the direct intervention of God because of his failure to repudiate the divine honors which the populace paid to him. Although Roman rulers were not infrequently deified, Herod Agrippa I was a nominal Jew, an exponent and defender of Judaism. Thus his culpability was great.

His death occurred in connection with an oration he gave

---

[35]If the events in Gal. 2 are in chronological sequence, then Peter's visit to Antioch would be considerably later than the time of Acts 12:17 (A.D. 44), since its mention in Galatians follows the account of Paul's trip to Jerusalem which was either the Famine Visit (A.D. 45, 46) or the Jerusalem Conference Visit (A.D. 49).

[36]The Greek term *apachthēnai* commonly meant "put to death," but sometimes means "led away to prison." F. F. Bruce suggests the translation "led away to punishment," but reminds us that in all likelihood that punishment was death, *The Book of Acts,* p. 253, ftn. 17.

[37]Although Caesarea was the capital of the Roman province of Judea, 12:19 seems to place it outside. Luke apparently is using "Judea" in the old tribal sense rather than as the Roman political term.

regarding the settling of a dispute between himself and the Phoenician cities of Tyre and Sidon. Herod had placed an economic embargo on foodstuffs to these cities, and perhaps the opening stages of the famine were being felt. Through the good offices of Blastus, the king's chamberlain,[38] Herod's wrath was cooled and he took the occasion of a festival at Caesarea to announce his good intentions. Josephus has a parallel description which agrees in essential points. He describes how Agrippa was struck with severe abdominal pain and was carried into the palace where he died five days later.[39] The expression "eaten of worms,"[40] is similar to Josephus' description of the death of Herod the Great,[41] and of the death of Antiochus Epiphanes mentioned in II Maccabees 9:9.

The return of Barnabas and Saul is placed here because their visit probably did not occur until A.D. 45, 46 after Herod's death. A textual problem occurs at verse 25, where some important manuscripts say "to Jerusalem"[42] instead of "from Jerusalem."[43] The sense of the passage demands that "from Jerusalem" be understood. John Mark came with the two emissaries, who perhaps had stayed at his mother's home while they were in Jerusalem.

QUESTIONS FOR DISCUSSION

1. Does conversion to Christ automatically remove a person's prejudices? If not, why not?
2. What does Peter's vision on the housetop indicate about the observance of the Mosaic food laws?
3. Does Acts 10:35 teach salvation by works?
4. What is the basis on which people receive the Holy Spirit?
5. Why do you think God delivered Peter from prison but did not deliver James?

---

[38]The Greek expression is *ton epi tou koitonōs tou basileōs*, "the one in charge of the king's bedchamber." In OT times it denoted the keeper of the harem. Here it refers to one in charge of the king's living quarters, thus one who had considerable access to the ruler's presence.

[39]*Antiquities of the Jews* XIX.8.2.

[40]Greek: *skōlēkobrōtos*.

[41]*The Jewish War* I.33.5; *Antiquities of the Jews* XVII.6.5.

[42]Particularly Aleph and B.

[43]Supported by P[74] and A.

THE WESTWARD ADVANCE:
ASIA MINOR, GREECE, AND ROME
Acts 13—28

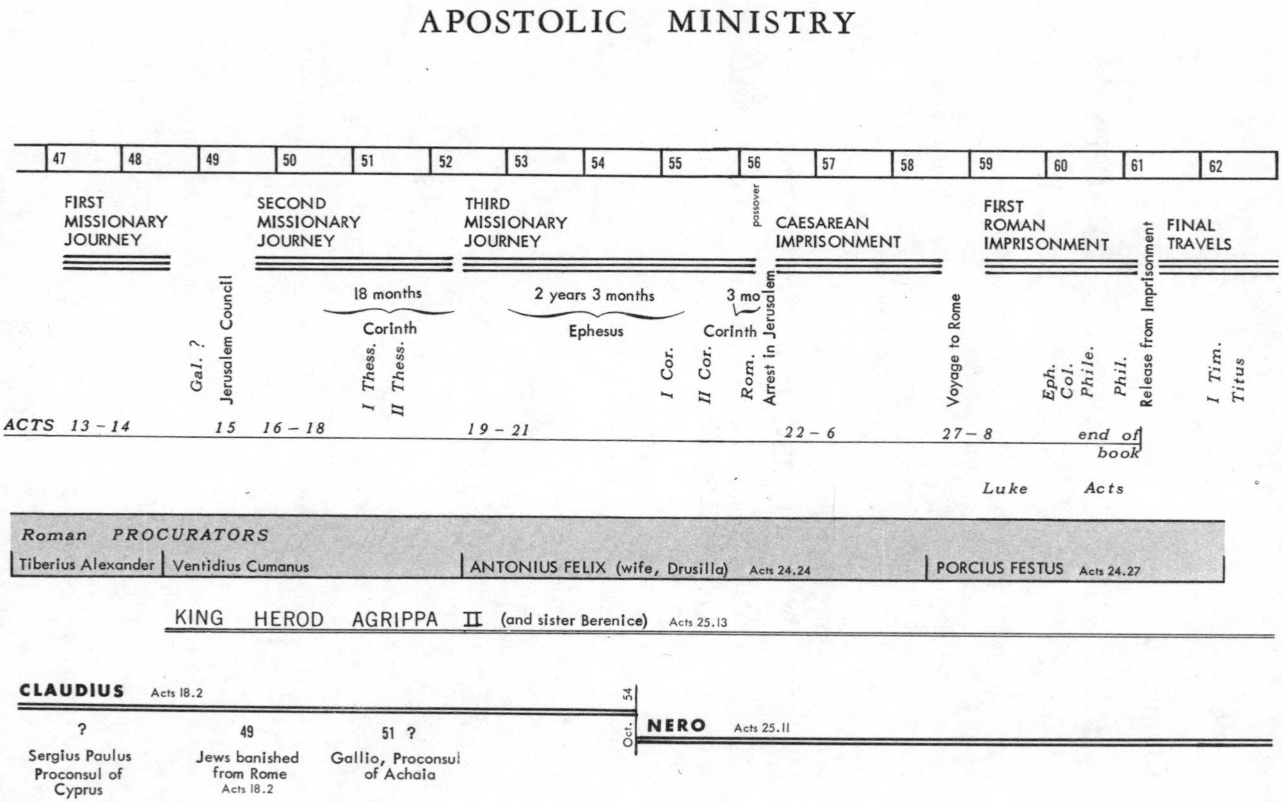

Fig. 11. Time Chart II: A.D. 47-62

Chapter 7

PAUL'S FIRST MISSIONARY JOURNEY
(Acts 13, 14)

At this point Luke has reached a significant moment in his history of the apostolic church. In the previous sections of his narrative, Palestine has been the scene of the activity, first at Jerusalem and then throughout the land, and Peter has been the most prominent figure.[1] Now the base of operations moves to Antioch in Syria, and Paul is the center of attention. This does not imply that the Jerusalem church became weak or lethargic, but it does indicate that as apostles carried out their various ministries, the significant activity for the historian's interest lay elsewhere. Luke has given us in the remainder of his book the exciting story of Paul's mission. As the great apostle to the gentiles, Paul's tireless efforts to make Christ known where others had not carried the message claimed the attention of our author.

I. THE CALL (12:1-3)

In the church at Antioch, in addition to those prophets who visited from Jerusalem (11:27), there were five resident prophets and teachers. Barnabas had been associated with the Antioch church almost from its beginning (11:22), and Saul had been brought in to assist shortly after (11:25, 26). Simeon (a Jewish name) was also called Niger, a Latin name meaning "black."[2] Lucius of Cyrene had a Latin name, and originally came from North Africa. Perhaps he is the same person who is mentioned in Romans 16:21. There is no good reason to identify him with

---

[1] In Acts 1-12 Peter is mentioned by name in every chapter except 6 and 7, and may have been the spokesman in 6:2. In the succeeding chapters, however, he appears only in Chapter 15.

[2] The nickname could suggest he was of dark complexion, and it is tempting to suggest he was from Africa and was the same as Simon of Cyrene (Mark 15:21). However, the fact that another in the group is said to be from Cyrene would seem to suggest that Simeon was not.

Luke the author. Manaen is called *suntrophos* of Herod the tetrarch.[3] The term means "companion" and was a title of honor given to boys who were reared at court with princes as their companions in education.[4] These five men with highly varied backgrounds had been transformed by the power of the gospel and now served the Lord together in the church at Antioch.

In the course of their ministry the Holy Spirit picked out Barnabas and Saul for a special task. The Spirit's revelation probably came as a direct inspiration to one or more of the prophets mentioned. Apparently Barnabas and Saul had already known the Spirit's will,[5] but they did not act unilaterally, apart from the church's knowledge and blessing.

Fasting was a part of the practice at Antioch among the leaders (13:2) as well as all the believers (13:3). Pious Jews of the time fasted twice each week, and early Christians may have continued the custom. The Mosaic Law commanded one annual fast (on the Day of Atonement).[6] Fasting is nowhere in the Bible commanded for Christians, although it is clear that some Christians voluntarily did so.[7] Fasting was coupled with prayer and the imposition of hands upon the two missionaries. This ritual was not an ordination in the sense of conferring special apostolic authority, for there were no apostles present to perform the rite (except Saul himself who was a recipient). It was rather the recognition by the church that God had called them, and it symbolized the identification of the Antioch church with these workers and the bestowal of their blessing.

II. THE JOURNEY (13:4–14:26)

A. *Cyprus* (13:4-13)

From Syrian Antioch the party proceeded to the seaport of Seleucia and embarked for the island of Cyprus (the home of

---

[3]Herod Antipas, murderer of John the Baptist.

[4]G. Adolf Deissmann, *Bible Studies* (Edinburgh, 1901), pp. 310-312.

[5]The perfect tense form *proskeklēmai*, "whereunto I have called them," indicates an act previously accomplished.

[6]Lev. 16:29, 31, where the phrase "afflict your souls" refers to fasting. See also Acts 27:9.

[7]Paul refers to his own fasting in II Cor. 6:5 and 11:27, but these occasions may have been forced upon him. See also Acts 14:23.

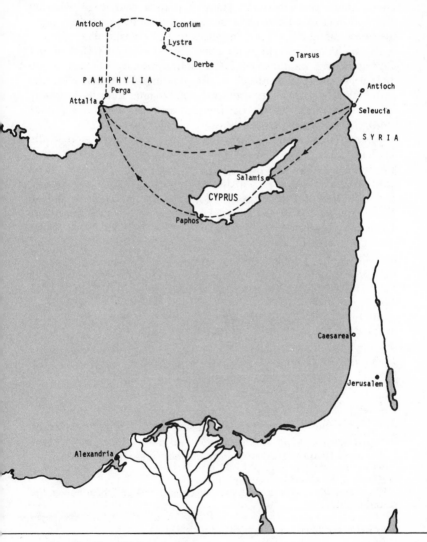

Fig. 12. First Missionary Journey

Barnabas, Acts 4:36). They landed at Salamis, a coastal city on the eastern side of the island, and here they undertook a synagogue ministry, a practice which would characterize their missionary procedure henceforth. The Jewish colony at Salamis was considerable inasmuch as the city had more than one synagogue. It must be remembered that the gospel had already reached Cyprus, so that there could have been a nucleus of believers already on the island (11:19). Although the fact is not directly stated, the mention of going through "the whole island" (13:6)[8] could imply that the policy of synagogue preaching was followed in other centers besides Salamis.

John Mark accompanied Barnabas and Saul in a subordinate capacity. He was not mentioned in 13:1-3, a fact which indicates his secondary position in the group, and thus his return later to Jerusalem was not disastrous. He could have been very helpful as a resource person for the events of Christ's life, inasmuch as neither Barnabas nor Saul had been companions of Jesus, and it is at least possible that Mark had some first-hand knowledge of Christ's life.

Making their way westward across the island, the missionary party came to Paphos, the capital on the western coast. Here they met Bar-Jesus, also called Elymas or sorceror. He was a Jew who falsely claimed to be a prophet of God, and apparently had ingratiated himself into the favor of the proconsul Sergius Paulus as some sort of advisor. He resented the interest which the proconsul was showing in the Word of God as preached by Barnabas and Saul. The Holy Spirit came upon Saul with a fresh filling[9] to enable him to perform a miracle of judgment upon Bar-Jesus. The physical blindness he experienced was appropriate to his spiritual condition.

Sergius Paulus is termed a proconsul,[10] rather than a propraetor, an indication that Cyprus was now a senatorial rather than an imperatorial province. Several inscriptions have been found which may refer to this man. Although there are serious

---

[8]Greek: *holēn tēn nēson.*

[9]Greek: *plēstheis.* The aorist participle denotes a fresh filling, in contrast to the adjective *plērēs* which denotes the character of a Spirit-filled man (cf. 11:24).

[10]Greek: *anthupatoi.*

problems concerning identification of the Sergius Paulus of Acts 13 with either the Proconsul Paulus of the Soli inscription, or the one mentioned by Pliny, the reference to L. Sergius Paullus in the *Corpus Inscriptionum Latinarum* remains a possibility.[11] The proconsul heard the gospel from the missionaries, witnessed the display of divine power in the miracle, and believed what he had seen and heard. Although no mention is made of his receiving the Spirit or of being baptized, this is no indication that these things did not occur. Nor should they cause us to question the validity of the proconsul's belief. William Ramsay has marshalled evidence to show that at least in later years a daughter and other descendants of this proconsul were Christians.[12]

It was at Paphos that Luke tells his readers that Saul is "the one also called Paul."[13] It was customary in bilingual countries for persons to have two names. Luke does not say that Paul at this point adopted the name. He doubtless had both names from childhood. Previously in predominantly Jewish surroundings the name "Saul" had been used. Now in a gentile governor's court it was likely that the apostle had introduced himself by the name "Paul," and the author uses this name consistently in the rest of the book because Paul from here on is primarily ministering as the apostle to the gentile world.

When the ministry on Cyprus was finished, the missionary party sailed to Pamphylia in Asia Minor. When they reached the city of Perga, John Mark abandoned the party and returned home (15:38). No reason is given although many have been suggested. Whether it was due to homesickness, resentment of Paul's elevation over his kinsman Barnabas,[14] or disagreement over the policy of gentile evangelization, cannot be determined, although Paul himself regarded it as serious (15:38, 39). Later,

---

[11]For a concise discussion of the problem, see *The Beginnings of Christianity,* Part I, Vol. V, ed. F. J. Foakes-Jackson and Kirsopp Lake (Grand Rapids, reprinted 1966), pp. 455-459.

[12]*The Bearing of Recent Discovery on the Trustworthiness of the New Testament* (Grand Rapids, reprinted 1953), pp. 150-172.

[13]Greek: *ho kai Paulos.*

[14]At the beginning it was "Barnabas and Saul" (13:2, 7); now it is "Paul and his company" (13:13).

however, Mark proved himself as a faithful servant of Christ, and a useful aide to Paul (II Tim. 4:11).

B. *Pisidian Antioch* (13:14-52)

1. *The Arrival* (13:14, 15)

Paul and Barnabas went from Perga to Pisidian Antioch[15] (not "Antioch in Pisidia," for Antioch is not in Pisidia but in Phrygia). This unusual way of referring to the city is paralleled by the first century writer Strabo who speaks of "Antioch near Pisidia." Apparently some such designation was necessary to distinguish the many cities named Antioch. "In passing from Perga to Pisidian Antioch, the travellers passed from the Roman province Pamphylia to the Roman province Galatia, and the rest of their journey lay in Galatia until they returned to Perga."[16] "Not until the Province Pisidia was formed about A.D. 295 was Pisidian Antioch in any strict sense a city of Pisidia. Under the Romans it was geographically a city of Phrygia, politically a city of the Province Galatia."[17]

Paul later wrote a letter to the churches of Galatia in which he mentioned a physical affliction that had caused him to preach there at the beginning.[18] Ramsay argues that an attack of malaria could have forced Paul from the lowlands of Perga without preaching to the higher altitudes of Pisidian Antioch (elevation 3600 feet).[19]

It was customary for synagogue rulers to invite visiting rabbis to speak. Once Paul's identity was known as the student of the celebrated Gamaliel, he would be most welcome.

2. *The Sermon* (13:16-41)

This was the first of Paul's sermons to be recorded in any

[15]Greek: *Antiocheian tēn Pisidian.*

[16]William M. Ramsay, *St. Paul the Traveller and the Roman Citizen* (Grand Rapids, reprinted 1949), p. 92.

[17]William M. Ramsay, *The Cities of St. Paul* (Grand Rapids, reprinted 1949), p. 254.

[18]Gal. 4:13, "You know that because of [Greek: *dia* with the accusative] weakness of the flesh I preached the gospel to you at the first."

[19]*St. Paul the Traveller*, p. 93.

detail. It is similar to Stephen's in its employment of historical restrospect (a speech which Paul probably heard), and also is not unlike Peter's sermon at Pentecost in its interpretation of certain OT passages (e.g., Ps. 16). The audience was composed of Jews and God-fearing gentiles (proselytes of the gate).

Paul's message demonstrated first that Jesus was the Messiah as promised to David (13:17-23). He traced Jewish history, and God's activity in guiding the nation, and brought this to a focus in their illustrious King David. Jesus, he said, was the descendant of the Davidic line, and was the fulfilment of the promises made to Israel.

The mention of 450 years (13:19, 20) should be construed with what precedes rather than with what follows. It apparently was a round number covering the sojourn in Egypt (approximately 400 years), the wilderness period (40 years), and the conquest of Canaan (rounded off as 10 years).[20]

The next section of Paul's sermon explained that Jesus is the Savior as foretold by the prophets (13:24-37). He showed how John the Baptist had testified to Jesus' coming (vss. 24-26). He explained that the rejection of Jesus by the Jewish authorities actually fulfilled the ancient prophecies (vss. 27-29). The crowning proof was the resurrection, which was also related to OT prophecy (vss. 30-37). Paul cited Psalm 16, and demonstrated that it must have been Messiah who was being referred to, not David himself, using the same argument as Peter did (2:25-31). In quoting Psalm 2:7, "This day I have begotten thee" (13:33), Paul interprets it of Christ's resurrection. In his view it was the resurrection which first fully declared Christ to be the Divine Son, since he now had his glorified body (Rom. 1:4).

The message closes with an appeal and warning (13:38-41). Paul challenges his hearers to receive forgiveness of sins through faith. In verse 39 Paul did not mean that the Mosaic Law provided divine justification for some sins, and Christ provides for the remainder. He meant rather that justification comes only

---

[20]This is the way it is treated in NASB. To regard the figure as denoting the time of the judges (so KJV) raises serious chronological difficulties, for that period was closer to 300 years than 450. See the chart "Patriarchs and Judges" by John C. Whitcomb, Jr., Winona Lake, Indiana.

by faith, not by works of law (Gal. 3:11), for animal sacrifices
per se could not remove sin (Heb. 10:4). Those who trusted in
Moses alone would find in the judgment that they had no real
forgiveness with God at all. Faith was necessary even in the
OT period. The good news revealed in Christ is that man's debt
has been paid by Christ's death, and full forgiveness is available
to all who will trust him for it.

3. *The Results* (13:42-52)

A favorable impression was made by the missionaries, and
arrangements were made for them to speak on the next sabbath.[21] Many of the Jews and proselytes followed Paul and
Barnabas, presumably to their lodging place, to hear more. The
expression "religious proselytes"[22] (13:43, KJV) occurs only
here in the NT. Whether it denotes full proselytes (as the term
proselutos alone normally does) or proselytes of the gate (as
the term *sebomenos* commonly did) cannot be determined with
certainty.

On the next sabbath a great crowd congregated to hear Paul
preach the Word of God. Among them were many gentiles who
were not even proselytes in any sense and this greatly agitated
the Jewish leaders. In their jealous zeal to protect their ancestral
faith they blasphemed by speaking against the truth about
Christ. As a result Paul and Barnabas announced, "Lo, we turn
to the gentiles" (13:46). This marked a definite break from their
previous evangelizing through the synagogue. Yet the missionaries knew that Scripture was on their side (Isa. 49:6). Although the majority of the Jews rejected the message, many of
the gentiles responded with joy and faith. All who responded
were, in fact, those who were appointed for eternal life. Once
again the human responsibility of believing is shown to coin-
cide exactly with what God in his sovereignty had planned.

The unrepentant Jews, however, did not cease their opposition. They persuaded the women proselytes who were socially
prominent in the city, along with the leading men of Antioch
(husbands of these women?), to use their influence in having

---

[21]Verse 42 does not contain the words "Jews" or "gentiles" in the best
manuscripts. The KJV reader should substitute "they" for each of those terms.

[22]Greek: *tōn sebomenōn prosēlutōn.*

Paul and Barnabas expelled from Antioch. Shaking off the dust of their feet as a gesture of disapproval (in the manner Jesus had instructed his followers, Luke 9:5; 10:11), the missionaries went to Iconium, a city eighty miles distant.

C. *Iconium* (14:1-6a)

The great crisis of turning to the gentiles outside the synagogue was now past (13:46), but this did not mean that Paul and Barnabas would henceforth ignore the synagogue. At Iconium they followed the same procedure of going first to the synagogue to give Jews the opportunity of hearing the gospel. There was, of course, a practical matter involved. If they had begun evangelizing among gentiles first, the synagogue would have been closed to them. The Lord blessed their labors with a multitude of converts and with the power to perform miracles.

Unbelieving Jews soon began their opposition, and eventually were able to enlist gentile supporters in their campaign against the two missionaries. The start of the opposition is stated in 14:2 and its climax in 14:5. While it was developing, the gospel continued to be preached until violence was about to break out. The attempt at stoning was hardly a plan for legal execution, but was most likely an effort to form a mob that would pelt the preachers with stones. Awareness of the plot caused Paul and Barnabas to flee twenty miles to Lystra.

The plural form "apostles"[23] is used in 14:4 (and vs. 14) of Paul and Barnabas. This is the first time Barnabas has been so designated. Usually this title is reserved in the NT for those directly chosen by Christ himself — the Twelve and Paul (with Matthias understood as a replacement for Judas). However, the word *apostolos* is used in the sense of a messenger authorized by a certain church in Philippians 2:25. Barnabas then may be understood as an apostle in the wider sense, either as a duly-recognized messenger (along with Paul) from the church at Syrian Antioch (13:2, 3), or as a member of an apostolic party (with Paul's apostleship in a sense lending its authority to Barnabas).

---

[23]Greek: *tois apostolois.*

D. *Lystra* (14:6b-20)

By fleeing to Lystra and Derbe, the travellers entered the region of Lycaonia, the implication of the author being that they crossed a border from Phrygia to Lycaonia in so doing. Luke has noted the fact, probably because the travellers were passing beyond the jurisdiction of the authorities at Iconium and should have reached a place of safety. Luke's accuracy was once severely challenged on this point because abundant records exist showing that Iconium was also a Lycaonian city, and thus no border would have been crossed between Iconium and Lystra. It was careful study of this matter which changed the British scholar William Ramsay into a strong defender of Luke's accuracy when he discovered that Iconium was Lycaonian earlier and again later, but that Luke's statement "was accurate at the period when Paul visited Lycaonia; that it was accurate at no other time except between 37 and 72 A.D."[24]

Luke has chosen for his history three incidents from the visit to Lystra: the healing of an impotent man, the strange episode of pagan superstition, and the stoning of Paul.

No mention is made of a synagogue at Lystra, although this city was apparently the home of Lois, Eunice, and Timothy (16:1; II Tim. 1:5).[25] These people may have been converted at this time, even though the fact is not mentioned. At Paul's visit on his second journey, Timothy already had a fine Christian reputation (16:2).

The miraculous healing of a man crippled in his feet produced a startling reaction. The excited populace reverted to their native tongue (doubtless Paul had been speaking in Greek) and identified the missionaries as divine visitors, Barnabas being called Zeus and Paul Hermes.[26] The Roman poet Ovid (43 B.C. A.D. 17) records the ancient myth concerning a visit of Zeus

---

[24]*St. Paul the Traveller*, pp. 110, 111; see also Ramsay, *The Bearing of Recent Discovery*, pp. 35-52.

[25]Although it is not stated directly that Timothy was from Lystra, Acts 16:1, 2 relates him either to Lystra or Derbe, and the enumeration in 20:4 mentions Gaius and Timothy in such a way as to imply that although Gaius was from Derbe, Timothy was not.

[26]The KJV has translated these Greek names by their Latin equivalents Jupiter and Mercury.

and Hermes to the neighboring region of Phrygia, disguised as mortals.[27] All turned them away except one old couple, Philemon and Baucis, on the Lycaonian border. Later a flood came in judgment and drowned all except this couple. Apparently the people at Lystra wanted no repetition, for the priest of Zeus whose temple was just outside the city began preparations for offering a sacrifice to their supposed divine visitors. Because all of the arrangements were being made in a language unknown to Paul and Barnabas, it was only at the last moment that the missionaries realized what the commotion was all about, and were able to get it stopped.

Paul's speech to these pagans was appropriate to his audience. He made no appeal to the Scripture, but built upon the knowledge they had from the natural world (Rom. 1:19, 20). He stressed the evidence in nature of a supernatural Creator, and showed the folly of idolatry. His message was successful in stopping the pagan sacrifice which was about to be made in their honor.

Disillusioned fanatics are easily led off into contradictory actions. After an interval of unstated length, Jews from Pisidian Antioch and Iconium, not content with expelling Paul from their own cities, persuaded those at Lystra to stone him. Again it was a mob-type stoning, not a legal action.[28] Dragging Paul outside the city, they left him for dead, but as the disciples stood by, perhaps making plans for a reverent burial, Paul got up and went back to the city, and the next day journeyed thirty miles to Derbe. Some have asserted that Paul actually died from this stoning and was resurrected.[29] Sometimes II Corinthians 12:1-9 is identified with this incident.[30] However, it should be noted that Luke is careful not to say that Paul was dead, but only that the Jews were supposing that he was dead. Furthermore, the incident mentioned in II Corinthians 12 does

[27]*Metamorphoses* VIII, 626ff.

[28]F. J. Foakes-Jackson reminds us: "It would have required a regular Hebrew court to sanction it [a legal stoning], and it would never have been tolerated in a Roman colony." Lystra was a Roman colony like Philippi (Acts 16:12). *The Acts of the Apostles* (London, 1931), p. 128.

[29]J. Rawson Lumby, *The Acts of the Apostles*, p. 264.

[30]H. A. Ironside, *Lectures on the Book of Acts* (New York, 1943), pp. 341-342.

not fit here chronologically, for the visit to Lystra occurred in
A.D. 47 or 48, and II Corinthians was written in A.D. 55 (see
Time Chart II). Yet Paul's experience of being caught up to
the third heaven was fourteen years prior to the writing of II
Corinthians. (Even if the time could be adjusted, Paul himself
didn't know whether he had died or not: "Whether in the body
or out of the body, I cannot tell," II Cor. 12:2, 3.) Nevertheless
a supernatural strengthening must have occurred in order for
Paul to recover as rapidly as he did.

E. *Derbe and Return* (14:21-26)

The ministry at Derbe was blessed with many converts. It
must have been more peaceful than the previous cities visited.
Derbe was the home of Gaius who later became a companion
of Paul (20:4). From Derbe it would have been closer and
probably safer to return to Syria by continuing eastward
through Tarsus. However, the missionaries retraced their steps
so as to assist the new churches they had established. This confirming ministry involved warning the believers that tribula-
tions are expected in this world. Paul had just experienced some
of these himself.

In each church they visited the believers were organized by
the choosing of elders. The word "ordained"[31] (14:23) translates a Greek term that originally meant to elect by a vote of
raised hands. The word also developed the more general sense
of "choose" or "appoint," as the compound verb[32] in Acts 10:41
indicates. Does 14:23 mean that Paul and Barnabas appointed
the elders for each church, or does the more restricted meaning
prevail with the sense that the missionaries established elders
in the churches by arranging for congregational elections? Although there is no question but that the term is capable of
either meaning, the following factors favor the interpretation of
an election:[33] (1) The choice of the verb *cheirotoneō* rather

---

[31]Greek: *cheirotonēsantes.*

[32]Greek: *procheirotoneō.*

[33]This view is held by William Ramsay, *St. Paul the Traveller*, pp. 121,
122; R. C. H. Lenski, *Interpretation of the Acts of the Apostles* (Columbus,
1944), pp. 585, 586; John Gerstner, "Acts," *The Biblical Expositor* (Phila-
dephia, 1960), III, 210.

than one of the many general words for "appoint" suggests that
the special characteristics of this word should be understood.
(2) The only other NT use of this exact verb is clearly with the
sense of a congregational selection (II Cor. 8:19). (3) Congregational selection was the apostolic practice in the choice of
the Seven (Acts 6:3).

When the travellers came to Pamphylia, they preached in
the city of Perga (no mention was made of any preaching there
on the outward journey). Then embarking from the port of
Attalia, they bypassed Cyprus and sailed directly to their home
base at Syrian Antioch.

III. THE REPORT (14:27, 28)

What a thrilling meeting it must have been when the Antioch
church came together to hear the first report of their intrepid
missionaries! Everything was explained, including no doubt how
God had supplied their needs, directed them where to go, and
protected them in spite of many dangers. Of greatest interest,
however, was the news that God had blessed in the salvation of
gentiles. By "gentiles" the historian meant not only God-fearers
but also pagans who had been given the gospel beginning at
Pisidian Antioch (13:46).

Paul and Barnabas remained in Syrian Antioch for a considerable time. In all likelihood it was during this period that Paul
wrote the Epistle to the Galatians.

QUESTIONS FOR DISCUSSION
1. How did the Holy Spirit speak to the church at Antioch?
2. Did Sergius Paulus become a true Christian believer?
3. Why was the preaching to gentiles at Pisidian Antioch a turning point
   for the church?
4. Did Paul die at Lystra?
5. What principles of church organization can be learned from Paul's procedure on his return journey?

Chapter 8

THE JERUSALEM COUNCIL
(Acts 15:1-35)

Gentile salvation apart from circumcision and compliance with Mosaic Law had seemed assured after the conversion of Cornelius. Even the Jerusalem church, located at the very center of Judaistic observances, had been convinced that God was truly saving gentiles (11:18). Paul's first missionary journey, however, focused attention again on the matter, and perhaps additional Jewish converts had been made who did not share the broader outlook of their older Christian brethren.

It may have been the reports of Paul and Barnabas about the success of their preaching among gentiles in Cyprus and Asia Minor that brought up the problem again. It was one thing for a proselyte of the gate like Cornelius to be converted. There were only so many of such proselytes, and they did have a real sympathy for Jewish traditions. But Paul and Barnabas had been evangelizing ordinary pagans who had no attachment to the synagogue whatsoever. If this should go unchecked, it would be only a matter of time until gentiles would be a majority in the church, and Jewish Christians would become an ever-shrinking minority group (in fact, this is exactly what has happened). The very character of the church was faced with the prospect of profound change. The issue came to a head in the months following the return of Paul and Barnabas to Antioch. The decision that was finally made has left its mark upon the Christian church from that time to the present.

I. THE PROBLEM (15:1-3)

Certain men came from Judea[1] and began teaching the gentile

---

[1]These may have been the "certain from James" whose insistence on kosher foods at Antioch led Peter, who was visiting there at the time, to act inconsistently and incur the rebuke of Paul (Gal. 2:11-14). Peter, of course, did not really share the views of these men, and is shown in Acts 15 to have the same basic viewpoint as Paul. See F. F. Bruce, *The Book of the Acts,* pp. 298-405, for an excellent discussion.

Fig. 13. Antioch in Syria, with Mount Silpius in the background. This city was the home base for Paul's missionary journeys, and its church sent delegates to the Jerusalem Conference. Levant Photo Service

Christians at Antioch that without circumcision they were not even saved. It was not a mere matter of establishing good social relations with Jewish Christians. These men made it an issue that questioned the very salvation of gentile Christians, not only those at Antioch but also the gentile converts that Paul and Barnabas had won during their recent expedition.

It is no surprise that Paul and Barnabas entered into great debate with these Judaizing teachers. The Antioch church decided[2] to send a delegation, consisting of Paul and Barnabas and some others, to discuss this matter with the officials at Jerusalem. They had the proper spirit, regarding the church as a unity, and recognized that the outcome would affect Christians everywhere. This was no time for unilateral action. Besides, the

[2]No subject is expressed for the verb *etaxan* ("determined") in 15:2, and the Western text supplies "those who had come from Jerusalem" as the subject, thus implying that they ordered the delegation to appear at Jerusalem. This hardly seems in keeping with the spirit of the passage, and the better course is to infer that the third person form of the verb implies "they" to be the members of the Antioch church.

issue had been raised by men from Jerusalem (15:24), and
therefore it was the ethical thing to have the two churches
most immediately involved discuss the problem.

Their journey would have taken them through Sidon and Tyre,
and then through Samaria to Jerusalem. The party visited with
the Christians they met along the way. Phoenicia had been evangelized at about the same time as Antioch (11:19) and Samaria
(8:1, 4, 5). A primary topic of conversation at these meetings
was the conversion of the gentiles that Paul and Barnabas had
witnessed. This was the cause of rejoicing among all the believers they met without any significant exception until they arrived
in Jerusalem.

II. THE DISCUSSION (15:4-29)

A. *The First Session* (15:4, 5)

When the delegation from Antioch arrived, they were welcomed by the Jerusalem church, both by the general membership and by the apostles and elders. It was doubtless Paul and
Barnabas who are meant as declaring "all things that God had
done with them." The particular reference, of course, was to the
events of their missionary journey and the conversion of gentiles
without the requirement of circumcision.

The problem at issue was raised immediately at this opening
general session by certain Jerusalem Christians who belonged
also to the Pharisee party.[3] They insisted that every gentile
Christian needed to be circumcised and compelled to keep all
the Mosaic Law, just as any Jew. This had been their own background and was their continued practice, and they saw no
reason to exempt gentiles if the gentiles hoped to enjoy the same
salvation as Jews. It should be noted that circumcision was not
the only requirement they wished to impose. If that one demand
of the Mosaic Law were introduced, there was no way to be
consistent without insisting upon all the rest of its obligations.
These Christian Pharisees saw that clearly, and demanded that
appropriate action be taken.

---

[3]The text does not imply that they were ex-Pharisees. A Pharisee could
become a Christian without relinquishing his distinctive beliefs regarding
Scripture and theology (the same could not be said of the Sadducees).

B. *The Second Session* (15:6)

Rather than continue the discussion with the whole assembly, the Apostles and elders met privately with the delegation from Antioch to consider the problem. The transitions in the text are difficult to trace here. Although 15:6 clearly indicates a private session, 15:12 speaks of "all the multitude," and 15:22 mentions "the whole church," and it seems certain that the speeches recorded here were heard by the entire congregation. Nevertheless, the same men who made the key speeches were also a part of the smaller group which met privately and they must certainly have made the same points in the smaller session. It is the suggestion of this commentator that 15:6 refers to the private session in which the leaders discussed the issue and settled upon the procedure to be pursued in presenting the case to the whole congregation. Verses 7-29 then describe the general session which followed.

Many have interpreted Galatians 2:1-10 as Paul's own account of this private session.[4] Certain similarities between the two

---

[4]This is the viewpoint of Alford, Lenski, Lightfoot, Machen, Meyer, *et al.*

Fig. 14. The Old City of Jerusalem, site of the Jerusalem Conference. This view is from the Mount of Olives. Levant Photo Service

accounts make this viewpoint attractive. The same two churches, the same persons, the same problem, and the same exemption of gentile Christians from circumcision are discussed in both accounts. Nevertheless there are problems with this explanation, and many have adopted the view that Galatians 2:1-10 refers to Paul's Famine Visit, not the Jerusalem Council.[5] Favoring this interpretation are the following factors: (1) Galatians 2:1-10 is said to be Paul's second visit to Jerusalem since his conversion, and this is shown in Acts to be the Famine Visit of 11:30 and 12:25 (the first visit was in 9:26). (2) The Galatians 2 visit was made in response to Divine revelation. This agrees with the Famine Visit of Acts 11:27-30, but there is no record of a revelation for Acts 15. (3) No mention is made in Galatians about the decisions of the Council, a fact which would certainly have aided Paul's argument in that passage. To this writer it seems better, therefore, to understand that Galatians was written from Antioch after the first missionary journey and after the problem of Judaizing had been introduced in Galatia and in Antioch, but shortly before the Jerusalem Council was held.

C. *The Third Session* (15:7-29)

1. *Peter* (15:7-11)

At this session the whole church was again involved (15:12, 22). After more discussion three speeches served to crystallize the issue and influence the final decision. Peter's comments built upon the Cornelius incident (10:1-48). He reminded the church that God had chosen him to preach to Cornelius, and that the Holy Spirit had been given at that time to uncircumcised gentiles just as to Jewish believers. It had been on the basis of faith, not any work of law, that salvation had been granted. To demand compliance with Mosaic regulations was to do something which God had obviously not done with Cornelius, and thus would be an act of presumption by the church. It would be to "tempt" God.

By referring to the law as a "yoke" which had been burdensome to themselves and to their ancestors, Peter used a concept similar to Galatians 5:1, "Be not entangled again with the yoke

---

[5]This position is held by Calvin, Ramsay, and F. F. Bruce.

of bondage." It has sometimes been objected that Peter's reference to the law as a burden does not fairly represent the attitude of first century Jews who found their "delight in the law of the Lord" (Ps. 1:2), nor is it consistent with Peter's self-confessed adherence to its traditions (10:14, 28). However, Peter is here expressing the attitude of Christ regarding the Pharisees' interpretation of the law (Matt. 23:1-4). F. F. Bruce reminds us that prior to A.D. 70 the severe school of Shammai was dominant in interpreting the law for the Jews, and the viewing of the traditional law as a great burden was characteristic of the ordinary Jew at this time.[6]

Peter ended his remarks with the reminder that even Jewish Christians are saved not by their observance of the Mosaic Law, but by the grace of God revealed in the Lord Jesus Christ. Hence it should not be thought strange that gentiles are saved the same way.

2. Barnabas and Paul (15:12)

The logic of Peter's argument silenced the opposition, and the audience gave full attention to Barnabas and Paul. These men, so recently returned from evangelizing in purely gentile areas, recounted the signs and wonders God had wrought among the gentiles. It should have been clear by these displays of God's approval upon their mission to gentiles that circumcision and compliance with the law was not a requirement for salvation.

3. James (15:13-21)

When Paul and Barnabas stopped speaking, James made the concluding speech and offered the recommendation which was adopted by the Council. This James was the Lord's half-brother (Gal. 1:19) who assumed increasing prominence in the Jerusalem church (12:17; 21:18).

James began by referring to Peter's remarks made earlier in the session. He called him "Simeon," the Semitic form of Simon (the same form used by Peter himself in II Peter 1:1). Peter had explained how he had been used of God for the first official incorporation of gentiles into the church in the incident of Cornelius. James now argues that this was in complete agree-

---

[6]See the concise discussion in F. F. Bruce, *The Book of the Acts*, p. 307.

ment with OT Scripture. He cited Amos 9:11, 12 with certain
variations (including additions) from the Hebrew and LXX
texts. The context in Amos speaks of judgment upon Israel and
the whole house of Jacob (Amos 9:7, 8), but holds out the
promise that "in that day" God will raise up the fallen royal
house of David and will restore his realm.

Interpreters have explained James' use of this prophecy in a
variety of ways.[7] (1) Some explain that James saw in the inclusion of gentiles in the church the fulfillment of Amos' words.[8]
This assumes that the NT church fulfills the OT prophecies regarding Israel. (2) Others explain that James merely finds the
principle of gentile salvation in Amos, and says that the present
policy of receiving gentile converts is thus not inconsistent.[9] A
weakness of this view is that the principle of gentile salvation
had always been accepted among the Jews. The point at issue
was whether it could be accomplished without Jewish ceremonies, and this interpretation offers no help with this problem.
(3) Still others interpret James as meaning that gentile salvation without circumcision meets with no contradiction in the
OT. The promises to Israel will yet be literally fulfilled, but
will occur "in that day" (i.e., when Messiah comes in glory).[10]
Inasmuch as that time is still future, James uses the phrase
"after these things" to indicate the relation of this prophecy to
God's present activity in the church. James also inserted the
words "I will return" to make it clear that fulfillment of Israel's
blessings must await Christ's return. This view has the advantage of treating the Amos prophecy literally, and thus main-
taining the distinction between Israel and the NT church. Amos
has shown what will occur in the future for Israel. Peter had
explained what God was doing in the meantime regarding salvation for gentiles.

James then offered his opinion[11] or resolution. He first con-

---

[7]A resume of views is given by Charles Zimmerman, "To This Agree the
Words of the Prophets," *Grace Journal*, Vol. 4, No. 3 (Fall, 1963), pp. 28-40.

[8]So Lenski, *Interpretation of the Acts of the Apostles*, pp. 608-611.

[9]F. W. Grant, *The Numerical Bible* (New York, n.d.), p. 100.

[10]Lewis Sperry Chafer, *Systematic Theology* (Dallas, 1948), IV, 267-269;
V, 328, 329.

[11]The verb *krinō* in 15:19 ("my sentence is," KJV) can denote James'
personal opinion, as its usage indicates in 4:19, 13:46, 16:15, and 26:8.

cluded that gentile converts should not be troubled by having any sort of Jewish ceremonies imposed upon them. He urged, however, that a policy of appropriate conduct be followed by gentile Christians. The reason for the latter was that Jews who were faithful to Moses were widely scattered throughout the gentile world, and gentile Christians should not unnecessarily offend them. Specifically there should be a refraining from pollutions of idols (explained in 15:29 as foods sacrificed to idols), fornication, and meats from animals that had been strangled and thus still contained blood. The prohibition regarding meat offered to idols is discussed by Paul in I Corinthians 8, where the same principle of respecting the other person's conscience is stressed. Because fornication is an evil *per se* and thus its prohibition is hardly to be understood as merely advice to avoid giving offense, some explain it as a reference to rules of marriage in Judaism (Lev. 18).[12] However, fornication was so widely practiced among pagans, even under the guise of religion, that an admonition to gentile Christians to pay particular attention to avoiding this sin was certainly not unwarranted.

4. *The Decision* (15:22-29)

James' recommendation was accepted by the other leaders and the church as a whole.[13] It was decided to relay the decision to Antioch by a delegation including two men of the Jerusalem church as well as Paul and Barnabas. This would alleviate any possible criticism that the results of the Council were unfairly reported by Paul. Of the two chosen from Jerusalem, Judas is not otherwise known to us. He has the same surname as Joseph Barsabbas, the other candidate with Matthias for the vacant apostleship (1:23), and it is commonly supposed they were brothers. Silas is apparently the same person who is called Silvanus in the epistles (II Cor. 1:19; I Thess. 1:1; II Thess. 1:1; I Peter 5:12).

A letter was also written "by them." The expression is literally

---

[12]Jackson, *The Acts of the Apostles,* p. 141.

[13]Jackson and Lake argue that *edoxe* ("it pleased," KJV) was a Greek technical term for voting or passing a measure in the assembly, and suggest the translation "it was voted" in 15:22. *The Acts of the Apostles,* IV, 178. Neither Arndt-Gingrich nor *TDNT* discuss this possibility.

"through their hand,"[14] and seems to imply that the four chosen men wrote it. However, this is more likely a Hebrew idom which denotes them as messengers, and in this instance as the agents who delivered the letter.[15] It was addressed to the Christian gentiles of Antioch (the city where the problem had been introduced) and the province in which Antioch was located, Syria and Cilicia (two regions which were administered as a single province under Syria until A.D. 72).[16] If it be questioned why Galatia was not mentioned, perhaps it was because the churches there were regarded as extensions of the work at Antioch, or else because the letter was merely sent to the church (and its environs) which had sent the delegation to Jerusalem.

The letter disavowed the teaching of the troublemakers at Antioch who had precipitated the whole problem. If they had come on some business from Jerusalem (Gal. 2:12), they had far exceeded their authorization and did not represent the attitude of the Jerusalem church on the matter of gentile relationship to the Mosaic Law. The letter further gave its clear approval to Paul and Barnabas, and supported the firm position they had previously taken at Antioch (15:2). The decisions reached at the Council were then listed.

It should be noted that the letter traced the unanimity of the decision to the action of the Holy Spirit (15:28), even though the Spirit was not mentioned previously as intervening in the proceedings. This is the way in which the Spirit usually works in the church. There need not be miraculous displays to indicate his direction. Spirit-filled people can detect his presence through the harmony which prevails when men are responsive to his will.

III. THE RESULTS (15:30-35)

The reading of the letter to the Antioch church caused great rejoicing. The status of the gentile converts was recognized as true salvation. Judas and Silas added their personal encouragement before returning to Jerusalem. Paul and Barnabas re-

---

[14]Greek: *dia cheiros autōn.*

[15]So Lumby, *The Acts of the Apostles,* p. 281; Jackson and Lake, *The Acts of the Apostles,* IV, 179, 180.

[16]E. M. B. Green, "Cilicia," *The New Bible Dictionary,* p. 233.

mained in Antioch to minister the Word, unhampered by any question about the salvation of their gentile believers.

Verse 34 is found in the Western text, and also in the Byzantine, but does not appear in the manuscripts usually regarded as most reliable.[17] Apparently it was thought that Silas had to be retained in Antioch in order to accompany Paul on the next journey, in plain contradiction of verse 33. There is no problem, however, if we understand a reasonable period of time between the events of verses 33 and 40, sufficient for Paul to send for Silas before the next journey.

QUESTIONS FOR DISCUSSION

1. What was the relation of the Jerusalem church to the church at Antioch?
2. Were Jews saved because they kept the Mosaic Law?
3. Did the Jerusalem Council impose Mosaic practices upon gentile Christians?
4. Why was it important for gentile Christians to avoid meat from animals that had been strangled?
5. How did the Jerusalem Council know that their decisions were prompted by the Holy Spirit as stated in their letter?

---

[17] Verse 34 does not appear in P[74] Aleph A B E P.

Chapter 9

PAUL'S SECOND MISSIONARY JOURNEY
(Acts 15:36—18:22)

The victory for gentile evangelization at the Jerusalem Council would naturally give added impetus to further spreading of the gospel. Furthermore, the Judaizing teaching which had so upset the church at Antioch had spread beyond that one city to at least as far away as Galatia, and reports of trouble in the churches so recently founded had come to Paul. These were doubtless some of the factors along with others that prompted Paul to think in terms of another missionary journey.

I. THE OPENING EVENTS (15:36 — 16:10)

A. *The Dispute with Barnabas* (15:36-41)

When Paul proposed such a trip to Barnabas, a sharp quarrel[1] followed because Barnabas was determined[2] to take John Mark again. Paul, however, thought Mark's previous defection rendered him unworthy (see 13:13). The result was that the two leaders separated. Barnabas took Mark with him to his homeland of Cyprus (4:36), and was perhaps instrumental in saving his young kinsman (Col. 4:10) for the ministry. Happily, the NT records that Paul was later reconciled to both men (Barnabas: I Cor. 9:6; Mark: Col. 4:10, Philem. 24, II Tim. 4:11). In the meantime God's providence overruled in securing two missionary teams instead of one. Inasmuch as we do not know the reasons for Mark's previous departure, we should be careful about assessing blame. Some may feel that Paul was a bit harsh at this point. However, it must be noted that the church officially approved Paul's new journey (15:40), although nothing is said about the trip of Barnabas.[3]

---

[1]Greek: *paroxusmos* (15:39).

[2]The verb in 15:37 *ebouleto* denotes a decision of the will after deliberation, and the imperfect tense indicates continued insistence.

[3]It should not be assumed that the church disapproved of Barnabas and

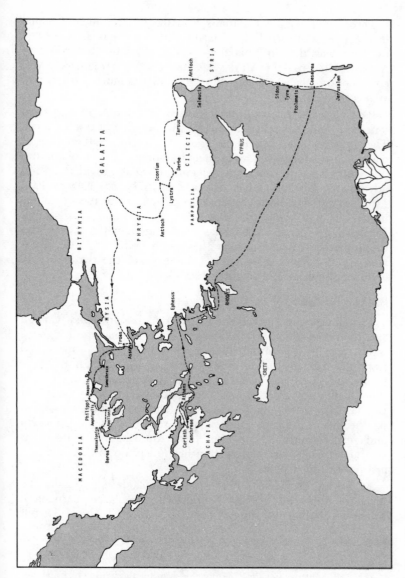

Fig. 15. Second Missionary Journey

Those who equate Galatians 2 with the Jerusalem Council face the difficulty that the quarrel with Barnabas as described by Paul was due to Judaizing (Gal. 2:13), but according to Acts was due to John Mark. The interpretation adopted in this commentary places the episode in Galatians much earlier, and avoids this problem.[4]

Paul chose Silas (who had returned to Antioch, or had been sent for), and they travelled overland through Syria and Cilicia. They visited churches throughout this region, although Acts contains no information as to their founding. In spite of the un-pleasantness at the start, the selection of Silas provided several advantages for Paul. Silas was a Roman citizen as was Paul (16:37) and thus both could claim citizenship to escape suffer-ing (it is not likely that Barnabas had Roman citizenship). Furthermore, inasmuch as Silas was named in the letter from the Jerusalem Council which they were delivering (15:27), it was appropriate that members from each of the two churches involved should be personally present.

B. *The Revisiting of the Churches* (16:1-5)

Travelling westward the two missionaries reached Galatia and the cities of Derbe and Lystra. These are named in reverse order from 14:6 because this time they were being approached from the east instead of the west. The cities of Galatia were given the decisions enacted by the Jerusalem Council, even though the official letter had been addressed only to Syria and Cilicia. The reason may have been that the churches founded on the first missionary journey were regarded as the extension and responsibility of the church at Antioch. These decisions reinforced what Paul had written in the Epistle to the Galatians just prior to the Council.[5]

At Lystra Paul met Timothy and enlisted him to take the place of John Mark (just as Silas had replaced Barnabas). Timothy's mother was Jewish (named Eunice, II Tim. 1:5), but

---

Mark, but at least one cannot conclude that the church sided with Barnabas against Paul.

[4]See comments on 15:6.

[5]This, of course, is not the only possible date for the writing of Galatians. Some would place it considerably later during the Third Journey.

his father was Greek.[6] Although his Jewish mother would have caused him to be regarded as a Jew, his lack of circumcision (by his father's influence probably) would cause Jews to reject him. Paul has been criticized for having Timothy circumcized in the light of the recent controversy at Jerusalem. However, it is clear that neither Paul nor Luke saw any inconsistency, for the very next sentence states that Paul conveyed the decisions of the Council. It should be remembered that the Jerusalem Council dealt with requirements for gentile converts, but Timothy was partly Jewish. Furthermore, this circumcision was not for salvation but was performed to make Timothy acceptable to synagogue audiences (not to placate Judaizing Christians). The operation regularized his status and increased his usefulness to Paul in Jewish areas.

C. *The Macedonian Vision* (16:6-10)

Passing through Galatic Phrygia[7] (in which were Iconium and Pisidian Antioch), and being directed by the Holy Spirit[8] not to preach at this time in the province of Asia nor in Bithynia, they passed through Mysia[9] and came to Troas. Here Paul had a vision in which a Macedonian man (whose nationality was indicated by his statement) urged him to come with his message of help. The vision was interpreted as meaning that God was directing the missionaries into Europe. In 16:10 there occurs the first of the so-called "we" sections of the book, and it is commonly assumed that the author Luke became a participant in the events at this time.

---

[6]The use of the Greek imperfect *hupērchen* ("was") in the indirect statement of 16:3 strongly suggests that his father was no longer alive. Otherwise a present tense would have been used.

[7]Greek: *tēn Phrugian kai Galatikēn chōran.*

[8]Luke's shift from the name "the Holy Spirit" in 16:6 to "the Spirit of Jesus" in 16:7 (Greek text, ASV) indicates no different Spirit. Inasmuch as the Spirit was sent by the Father and the Son (John 14:26; 16:7), he is variously referred to as the Spirit of God, the Spirit of Christ (Rom. 8:9), or the Spirit of Jesus.

[9]"Passed through" is a legitimate translation of *parelthontes* in 16:8 (so Arndt-Gingrich, *Greek-English Lexicon.*) It must have this meaning here inasmuch as Troas is in Mysia.

II. THE MAJOR CITIES (16:11 – 18:17)

A. *Philippi* (16:11-40)

1. *The Conversion of Lydia* (16:11-15)

A two-day voyage brought the party by way of the island Samothrace to Neapolis, the port utilized by Philippi. Sailing must have been with favorable winds inasmuch as a reverse journey took five days (20:6).

Philippi was the first European city in which Paul preached. It was located on the Egnatian Way, the Roman highway which connected the Aegean Sea with the Adriatic. The city had the status of a colony.[10] which meant that it had been organized by the state and was actually a military outpost. Sometimes colonies were settled by Roman army veterans. The people were given the rights of Roman citizens. The distinctive prerogatives of a colony were autonomous government, immunity from tribute and taxation (at least in some cases), and treatment as if they actually lived in Italy.[11]

Philippi is also called *prōtē*[12] ("first," "chief") of the district of Macedonia (16:12). It cannot mean it was the capital of the province of Macedonia, for Thessalonica held that distinction; nor can it mean the capital city of its district, for Amphipolis served in that capacity. Evidence exists from a later period that *prōtē* was an honorary title bestowed on certain cities, and this could be the explanation for Philippi.[13] It is more likely, however, that the absence of the article points simply to the meaning "a leading city" in that part of Macedonia.

Apparently there was no synagogue in Philippi, but the missionaries went outside the city on the sabbath where there was

---

[10]Other colonies named in Acts are Pisidian Antioch, Lystra, Troas, Corinth, Ptolemais, Syracuse, and Puteoli. Jackson and Lake, *The Acts of the Apostles*, IV, 190.

[11]A good discussion appears in Jackson and Lake, *The Acts of the Apostles*, IV, 187-190.

[12]The United Bible Societies text has adopted the conjecture *prōtēs*, so that the sense is "a city of the first district of Macedonia." This avoids the historical problem, but can claim no Greek manuscript support.

[13]See the evidence collected by Jackson and Lake, *The Acts of the Apostles*, IV, 187-189.

a Jewish prayer place.[14] The absence of men at the prayer place may explain why there was no synagogue in the city, for ten Jewish men were required for its establishment.

As Paul preached the first convert was a woman named Lydia from Thyatira (in Asia Minor). She was a God-fearer,[15] and responded fully to the gospel as the Lord opened her heart to understand. She was evidently a business woman who had settled in Philippi with a household of her own. Perhaps some of the women present at the meeting were her servants in her business of selling purple dye and cloth. Lydia showed her genuine conversion by receiving baptism and by graciously opening her home to the missionary party.

2. The Exorcism of a Demon (16:16-18)

Enroute to the prayer place the missionaries were accosted by a girl possessed of an evil spirit. The text says literally "having a spirit, a Python."[16] The name comes from the ancient Greek oracle at Delphi, a city which was also called Pytho because the god Apollo was alleged to be embodied in a snake there. Soothsayers (and even ventriloquists) were therefore called "Pythons." In this instance the girl was actually demon possessed. Her unsolicited testimony to the missionaries was abolutely true, and yet after putting up with it for many days Paul cast out the demon on the authority of Jesus Christ. Perhaps he saw that the results of this sort of testimony were not helpful but confusing to those who heard it. He was following the precedent of Jesus who always refused the testimony of demons, even though they spoke truth (e.g., Mark 1:23-25; Luke 4:41).

3. The Conversion of the Jailer (16:19-40)

The owners of the slave girl whose economic usefulness as a soothsayer had just vanished seized the two leaders Paul and Silas and took them before the magistrates in the city center.[17]

---

[14]The Greek word *proseuchē* can mean prayer or place of prayer.

[15]Greek: *sebomenē ton theon* (16:14), a phrase which denotes a gentile who had become a partial proselyte (proselyte of the gate).

[16]Greek: *echousan pneuma puthōna* (16:16).

[17]Greek: *agoran*, commonly translated "marketplace" (16:19).

A Roman colony was governed by two rulers called *duumvirs* or praetors.[18] Although the reasons for the seizure were economic, the charges made were religious and political. It was illegal for Jews to proselyte actively among Roman citizens, and special reference was made to the Roman status of the Philippians (16:21). This resulted in their being publicly stripped, beaten, and then imprisoned without trial. Instead of groaning over their wounds, the missionaries spent the night praying and singing, not unmindful that other prisoners were listening.

Luke has condensed much information regarding the events following the earthquake. Apparently the jailer saw from his quarters that the doors had been sprung open, and as he came to investigate, he decided on suicide in view of the inevitable punishment he would incur if the prisoners were gone (12:19). Paul, seeing him silhouetted in the doorway, dissuaded him by the news that the prisoners were still there. They may have been too frightened to leave, or may have been influencd by Paul to remain. Also their chains still dangled from their wrists (although torn loose from the wall by the earthquake), and recapture would have been fairly easy.

The jailer was tremendously impressed by these events. Whether it was the earthquake, the previous preaching of Paul in the city, or the conduct of Paul and Silas in the jail, or their cumulative effect, he desired salvation for himself. Paul lost no time in proclaiming his need for faith in the Lord Jesus Christ. The statement, "Thou shalt be saved and thy house," does not mean that his household would be saved automatically. The fact that the Word of the Lord was proclaimed to the whole household (16:32) shows that the belief required of the jailer was necessary for them too.

In the morning the authorities sent word to release the prisoners. Perhaps they connected the earthquake with Paul and Silas, as the jailer had done. Yet the missionaries refused to leave so unceremoniously. They had been illegally treated, without even an opportunity to claim their Roman citizenship previously. By insisting upon a dignified exit and the personal presence of the magistrates, they doubtless secured a measure

---

[18]See the discussion in Jackson and Lake, *The Acts of the Apostles,* IV, 194, 195.

of protection for the Philippian believers who might otherwise have suffered continued persecution.

Apparently Luke was left behind at Philippi to oversee the new work. At least the "we" is dropped at this point, and is not resumed until 20:5, 6 when Paul returns to Philippi on the Third Journey.

B. *Thessalonica* (17:1-9)

Departing from Philippi, Paul and his party travelled by the Egnatian Way one hundred miles to Thessalonica, capital of the province of Macedonia. Apparently nightly stops were made at Amphipolis (thirty-three miles from Philippi), Apollonia (thirty miles from Amphipolis) until they reached Thessalonica (thirty-seven miles from Apollonia). Jackson and Lake have an interesting comment at this point:

> . . . If this passage is taken to mean that the journey was really finished in three stages — which is its natural though not its necessary meaning — Paul must have used horses, and it is the best evidence I know to settle the question whether Paul always went on foot . . . or was in a position to hire horses.[19]

For three sabbath days Paul spoke in the synagogue. The verb "reasoned"[20] (17:2) indicates a discussion rather than a formal sermon. "Opening and alleging"[21] (17:3, KJV) suggests an exposition whereby the facts of gospel history were presented as evidence alongside the OT prophecies to show that Jesus was truly the predicted Messiah. Some of the audience believed including the Jew Aristarchus (Col. 4:10) and the God-fearing Greek Secundus (Acts 20:4). A number of socially prominent gentile women were affiliated with the synagogue and many of them also responded to the gospel.

Jealous Jews instigated the persecution. Perhaps they resented the loss of financial support from the wealthy women who had converted to Christ (17:4). They hired a band of marketplace loafers[22] and staged a riot in hopes of seizing the missionaries. Unable to find their quarry, they seized Jason their host, along

---

[19]*The Acts of the Apostles*, IV, 202.
[20]Greek: *dielexato.*
[21]Greek: *dianoigōn kai paratithemenos.*
[22]Greek: *agoraiōn*, from the word *agora*, marketplace.

with certain others, and took them to the city authorities called politarchs[23] (17:6). Although the charge of treason was serious, the politarchs did not seem terribly upset, perhaps because no real evidence was presented. Some sort of bond was demanded from Jason, making him responsible for the actions of the missionaries.

C. *Berea* (17:10-15)

Because the populace was so aroused at Thessalonica (and the bond Jason posted may have required Paul's departure), Paul and Silas (and Timothy, 17:15) left by night for Berea sixty miles away. The Berean Jews were much more generous-minded than those of Thessalonica. They received Paul's preaching eagerly, and then tested the gospel by comparing the message with the Scripture (always an admirable procedure). By doing this carefully and daily, many became Christian believers. Mention is made later of Sopater the son of Pyrrhus who was a Berean Christian (20:4, ASV).

Eventually Jews came from Thessalonica and began stirring up opposition. The Berean Christians hastily got Paul out of town, although Silas and Timothy remained in Berea for a time. Textual variations occur in the manuscripts at this point, making it uncertain whether Paul went to Athens by sea or by land. The fact that the Bereans conducted Paul to Athens favors the understanding that they travelled by land, and thus the Byzantine text is preferable. This reading suggests that the party went to the coast as though to go by ship (to throw pursuers off the track), and then went south to Athens by land.

C. *Athens* (17:16-34)

Athens was in the province of Achaia, and was the headquarters of Greek mythology. Most of its incomparable statuary had religious significance. As Paul waited for his companions he was more impressed (and depressed) by the idolatry reflected in the statutes than by their artistic excellence.

Paul's ministry in Athens included synagogue preaching and

---

[23]Greek: *politarchos*. This title has been found in numerous inscriptions from this period, including one inscribed on an arch at Salonika. The title refers to local magistrates of Macedonian cities.

daily encounters in the Agora with any he chanced to meet. Luke has picked out as the most significant event the address of Paul before the Areopagus. It began when Epicurean and Stoic philosophers[24] heard Paul in the marketplace. Epicureans sought contentment by a serene detachment from the world, and believed there would be no divine intervention in life nor punishment after death (the emphasis on sensual pleasure was a later perversion). They were materialistic in their outlook. Stoics sought happiness by accepting nature as it is and finding their place within it. They were essentially pantheistic. Some of these philosophers were unimpressed with Paul, calling him a "seed-picker."[25] Others recognized him as a religious teacher who was propounding strange deities (perhaps the plural indicates that they had mistakenly personified resurrection along with Jesus).

The Areopagus[26] was the same court which had tried and condemned Socrates centuries before. Sometimes it met on the hill west of the Acropolis. It was this hill that had lent its name to the Court itself. At other times the Court met in the Royal Stoa. Where it met to hear Paul is not certain, inasmuch as "Areopagus" can mean either the hill, the Court, or both. The power of this Court was greatly curtailed in democratic Athens and now dealt chiefly with moral and religious matters. In Paul's case, it was certainly no more than a hearing, inasmuch as he does not seem to be on trial and no verdict is pronounced.[27]

Paul's address took into full account the nature of his audience. He observed that they were unusually religious,[28] for he

---

[24]For a brief description of these two philosophies, see the articles in *The New Bible Dictionary*.

[25]Greek: *spermologos*. The term was used literally of birds, and figuratively of one who lived by picking up scraps, or as here of a vagrant philosopher who belonged to no recognized system.

[26]The translation of this term is "Hill of Ares" (Lat. equiv. "Mars").

[27]Ramsay states: "Now, certain powers were vested in the Council of Areopagus to appoint or invite lecturers at Athens, and to exercise some general control over the lecturers in the interests of public order and morality . . . The scene described in vv. 18-34 seems to prove that the recognized lecturers could take a strange lecturer before the Areopagus, and require him to give an account of his teaching and pass a test as to its character," *St. Paul the Traveller*, pp. 246, 247.

[28]Greek: *deisidaimonesterous*. The word can mean either "very superstitious" or "very religious." It is unlikely that Paul would have deliberately

had even found an altar dedicated TO AN UNKNOWN GOD.[29]
He used their admitted ignorance as a basis for his message
about the true God. Paul explained that God is the creator, the
sovereign of heaven and earth, the sustainer and director of all
things, and is the Omnipresent One.

Verse 26 states that mankind is of common descent from one
original man (i.e., Adam), and explains that God has determined
the seasons which make life possible, and has appointed the
habitable zones of the earth in which men may live. (This
could hardly mean that people must not migrate from one part
of the earth to another; otherwise most Americans should go
back to Europe, and Abraham should never have left Ur.)

Verse 28 is probably composed of two quotations. The first is
the last line of a stanza by Epimenides, from which Paul quoted
the second line in Titus 1:12. The second quotation is from
Aratus.

The message continued by pointing to the certainty of divine
judgment, and the necessity of repentance. The striking asser-
tion in the Athenians' view was the statement that the resurrected Jesus would be the judge. Some have said that this sermon was too philosophical and was not really the gospel. It
should be noted, however, that the message was interrupted,
and Paul was doubtless intending to enlarge upon the saving
work of Christ. Nevertheless, it did contain the core of the
gospel, for it condemned idolatry and sin (17:29), showed the
need of repentance (17:30), told of the certainty of judgment
(17:31a), and spoke of salvation through the One whom God
had raised from the dead (17:31b). The theological viewpoint
in the message is entirely consistent with Paul's teaching in
Romans 1-2.

The message resulted in conversions including Dionysius, a
member of the Areopagus Court, and Damaris, a woman not
otherwise known to us.

---

antagonized his audience at the outset, but the ambiguity of the expression
may have dictated its selection.

[29]Greek: *Agnōstōi Theōi*. Although no altar has been found at Athens with
this precise inscription, similar ones have been found elsewhere inscribed to
"unknown gods." See the thorough discussion by Kirsopp Lake, *The Acts of
the Apostles*, V, 240-246.

E. *Corinth* (18:1-17)

1. *Paul's Companions* (18:1-4)

Leaving Athens Paul made his way westward along the isthmus that connects the Pelponnesus with the mainland of Greece until he came the fifty-three miles to Corinth.[30] Corinth was the capital of the province of Achaia, and was a great commercial center. The city was served by two ports on the opposite sides of the four-mile-wide neck of land, Lechaeum on the northwest and Cenchraea on the southeast. To save the two hundred mile voyage around the Peloponnesus, traders often put their ships on rollers and moved them overland from one port to the other. Nero began constructing a canal in A.D. 67, but the Corinth Canal was not completed until 1893. Corinth was famed for its Temple of Aphrodite on its acropolis, in which one thousand sacred prostitutes contributed their sordid influence to the morals of the city.[31]

When Paul reached Corinth he stayed with Aquila and Priscilla. This couple is mentioned six times in the NT. They were apparently already Christians when Paul met them (at least their conversion is not mentioned here with the others, 18:8). They had recently come from Rome (where a church already existed, Rom. 1:7-8) because of the decree of Claudius. This decree, issued in A.D. 49,[32] was referred to by Suetonius as follows:

> . . . Because the Jews at Rome caused continuous disturbances at the instigation of Crestus, he expelled them from the city.[33]

It is commonly supposed that Suetonius was referring to riots in the Jewish community over the preaching of Christ, but that he has misspelled the name and has perhaps erroneously thought

---

[30]See the Article "Paul Departed from Athens and Came to Corinth," by Homer A. Kent, Jr., in *The Brethren Missionary Herald,* December 27, 1969, pp. 18, 19.

[31]F. F. Bruce reminds us: "In classical Greek, *korinthiazō* (literally "act the Corinthian") means to practice fornication; *Korinthiai hetairai* or *Korinthiai korai* ("Corinthian companions" or "Corinthian girls") are harlots," *The Book of Acts,* p. 367, fn. 4.

[32]A brief but careful discussion of the date can be found in Jackson and Lake, *The Acts of the Apostles,* V, 459, 460.

[33]"Claudius," XXV, *Twelve Caesars.*

that Christ was actually a rebel leader in Rome (Suetonius was
born in A.D. 69, and wrote considerably after the event).

Paul stayed with Aquila and Priscilla and engaged in labor
with them for they were all "tentmakers." The term *skēnopoioi*
was commonly used of leather-workers. The province of Cilicia
from which Paul came was noted for the production of a cloth
made from goats' hair called *cilicium*, and perhaps this was
Paul's manual skill.[34]

2. Paul's Ministry (18:5-11)

Paul at the first had been laboring at his trade during the
week and speaking in the synagogue each sabbath. When Silas
and Timothy came from Macedonia, they brought a gift which
freed him to devote more time to his missionary efforts (II Cor.
11:8, 9; Phil. 4:15). The movements of Silas and Timothy are
only partially recorded in Acts, and additional data must be
gleaned from the epistles. The following must have occurred:
(1) Silas and Timothy had been left behind at Berea with instructions to meet Paul at Athens (17:14, 15). (2) They did
meet Paul as planned (17:16; I Thess. 3:1). (3) From Athens
Timothy was sent to Thessalonica to encourage the church
(I Thess. 3:1, 2). Silas also must have gone to someplace in
Macedonia, perhaps Philippi (18:5). (4) Both men rejoined
Paul at Corinth, bringing a report from Thessalonica (I Thess.
3:6) and a gift (II Cor. 11:8, 9; Phil. 4:15). It was at this time
that Paul wrote First Thessalonians, and shortly after he probably wrote Second Thessalonians from Corinth also.

Paul's synagogue ministry had many favorable results. One of
the synagogue's rulers, Crispus, became a Christian along with
his household. He was one of the few whom Paul personally
baptized (I Cor. 1:14-16). When the synagogue preaching had
to be abandoned because of Jewish opposition, Paul established
his headquarters next door in a private home belonging to a
proselyte named Titius Justus.[35] It is possible that he was the
same man as Gaius, whom Paul terms his host at Corinth on the
Third Journey (Rom. 16:23). If so, his full name would be Gaius

---

[34]See Jackson and Lake, *The Acts of the Apostles*, IV, 223.

[35]This follows the reading of P[74] and B. Other manuscripts read Titus
Justus (Aleph, E), or simply Justus (A, D, Byzantine text).

Titius Justus, and he would have been another whom Paul personally baptized (I Cor. 1:14).

At crucial periods in Paul's life the Lord appeared to him. At Corinth the Lord knew the plot which was in store and encouraged him. Perhaps Paul was temporarily discouraged (I Cor. 2:3). By a vision the Lord informed him that he would not be harmed, and that his labors would be fruitful in Corinth. (Note that the Lord knew those who were his, even before they were converted, 18:10.) As a result Paul took courage and stayed in Corinth eighteen months.

3. *Paul before Gallio* (18:12-17)

Gallio, the proconsul of Achaia, was the brother of the philosopher Seneca. An inscription from Delphi shows that he was proconsul during the period A.D. 51-52 or 52-53.[36] It was at this time that the Jews seized Paul and took him to Gallio's tribunal. This was the first time that Paul (or any other apostle as far as we know) had been on trial before a Roman provincial governor. He was accused of activity contrary to the law (18:13). Whether they meant Jewish law or Roman law is not clear, and perhaps it is not necessary to separate the two. His accusers regarded him as teaching contrary to Judaism, and thus he was acting in a way not sanctioned by Roman law, for the Romans had granted Jews the right to practice their own religion and even to make converts (although not to proselyte among Roman citizens).

If Gallio had decided the case against Paul, this precedent would have been noted by other proconsuls. The missionary enterprise of the church could have been made vastly more difficult. Gallio, however, threw the whole case out of court, ruling that it was a religious dispute, and in no sense a crime under civil jurisdiction. He refused to concern himself and his court with the case.

When the case was dismissed, apparently the Jews did not

---

[36]Johannes Munck interprets the data as pointing to A.D. 51-52, but Jackson and Lake conclude A.D. 52-53. Assuming that the incident occurred near the end of Paul's visit and near the beginning of Gallio's term, Paul must have reached Corinth either in A.D. 49 or 50. Munck, *The Acts of the Apostles,* pp. 177, 178; Jackson and Lake, *The Acts of the Apostles,* V, 460-464.

Fig. 16. Ruins of the Bema at Corinth, where Paul appeared before Gallio. Photo by the author

immediately leave the scene. Gallio then ordered them driven out. The Jewish leader Sosthenes[37] must have been the most vocal, and was given a beating by those responsible for court-room order.[38] The *bēma* or tribunal where these events occurred may still be seen at Corinth.

III. THE RETURN TO ANTIOCH (18:18-22)

After continuing for a time at Corinth to make good use of Gallio's official "hands off" policy, Paul took a ship from Cench-raea (the home of Phoebe and location of another church, Rom. 16:1), travelling with Priscilla and Aquila. Apparently Paul had taken a Nazirite vow during his stay in Corinth and the period

[37]Sosthenes as synagogue ruler was either the successor or former colleague of Crispus (18:8). It is possible that he later became a Christian (I Cor. 1:1), but if so Luke takes no notice of the fact.

[38]The term "Greeks" does not appear in the best manuscripts at 18:17. The view assumed above is that those who beat Sosthenes were the same ones who drove the others from the Bema.

of the vow (usually thirty days) was now over.[39] Such vows are described in Numbers 6:1-21. At the conclusion of the vow one's hair was cut (or shaved) and burned with a sacrifice at Jerusalem. It must be remembered that Acts describes a period of transition, and it should not surprise us to find Christian Jews still observing Jewish ritual as a matter of choice.

Stopping off at Ephesus for his first visit there,[40] Paul did not remain in spite of a warm invitation to do so. However, Prescilla and Aquila did stay in Ephesus and became most helpful to the new Christians (see 18:26). The KJV follows the Western and Byzantine texts in giving Paul's reason for not remaining as his haste to reach Jerusalem in time for a feast (18:21). That particular statement does not appear in many ancient manuscripts including P[74], Aleph A, B, and E. However, it may well be the explanation for his departure, whether or not it belongs in the original text.

Leaving Ephesus, Paul's route took him to Caesarea, Jerusalem, and Antioch. Although Jerusalem is not mentioned by name in 18:22, it appears to be meant in the phrase "having gone up and greeted the church." The expressions "went up" and "went down" are so frequently used of going to and from Jerusalem as to be almost technical phrases. Furthermore, the expression "went down to Antioch" would be incorrect if referring to a journey from Caesarea to Antioch inasmuch as Antioch was inland while Caesarea was on the coast (one was always said to "go up" from the coast to an inland place). Thus ended Paul's first European tour. A more eventful and significant trip could hardly be imagined.

QUESTIONS FOR DISCUSSION

1. Was the dispute between Paul and Barnabas sinful? Who was right?
2. Why did Paul circumcize Timothy, especially so soon after the Jerusalem Council?
3. Why did Paul insist that the magistrates at Philippi come personally to release the missionaries?

[39]Grammatically, either Paul or Aquila could be the one whose hair was cut. Because Paul is the significant person in the narrative, it is generally understood that he was the one who took the vow.

[40]Paul had previously been forbidden by God to preach in Asia, of which Ephesus was the capital, but this restriction must now have been lifted (16:6).

4. Was Paul's sermon at Athens more a display of human wisdom than of spiritual power?
5. Why was Gallio's action important for the gospel?

Chapter 10

PAUL'S THIRD MISSIONARY JOURNEY
(Acts 18:23—21:16)

After a stay of indeterminate length at Antioch, Paul set out again on his third extended tour. Although this trip, commonly known as Paul's third missionary journey, occupied more time than his previous ones, it took Paul to no new areas. Thus it was more of an instructing and confirming mission than a pioneering venture. Luke's interest in the narrative clearly centers upon the events at Ephesus. He has mentioned Paul's brief stopover in 18:19-21, and then sketches in a few brief sentences the intervening events until Paul returns to Ephesus (19:1). A lengthy description is given of Paul's activity in the city (Chap. 19), and then a rather full report is included of his farewell address to the Ephesian elders (20:17-38). Other activities during this journey are mentioned with much brevity. Ephesus is clearly the place of major significance on the third journey.

I. THE PRELIMINARY MINISTRY OF APOLLOS (18:23-28)

Between Paul's two visits to Ephesus, Apollos came and ministered in the synagogue. He was an Alexandrian Jew who was a learned[1] and powerful expounder of the OT Scripture. He himself had previously been instructed in the way of the Lord, and was able to teach accurately many things regarding Jesus.[2] However, his information stopped short of the ministry of John the Baptist. Apparently he had come under the influence of a disciple of John, and had learned some of the facts of Jesus' life and ministry including his identity as the Lamb of God (John 1:29). He had never been taught concerning the finished work of Christ, Pentecost, and Christian baptism.

Aquila and Priscilla heard Apollos in the synagogue and took him aside to give him further enlightenment. It should be noted

---

[1]Greek: *logios*. The alternative meaning "eloquent" is also possible.

[2]The KJV rendering "things of the Lord" (18:25) is based upon an inferior reading. One should follow ASV here, based on P[74] Aleph A B E.

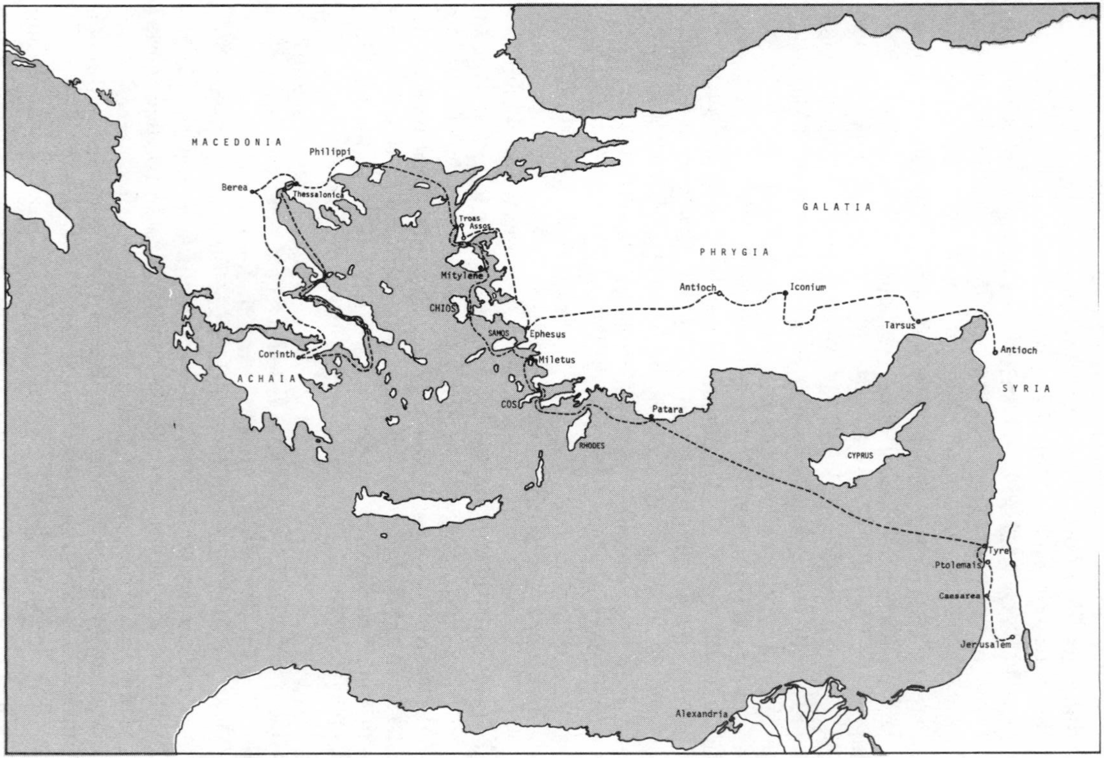

Fig. 17. Third Missionary Journey

that these two Christians still attended the synagogue (and Paul did as well on both of his visits to Ephesus). It is clear that at this transitional stage, the sharp break between synagogue and church was not yet made everywhere. The action of Aquila and Priscilla demonstrated the sort of Christian attitude that all would do well to follow. They did not criticize Apollos to others, but sought privately to aid him in correcting his incomplete message. Apollos responded well to this further light. When later he desired to visit the believers at Achaia (Corinth, 19:1), the Christians at Ephesus wrote a warm letter of recommendation for him. His ministry at Corinth became a very fruitful one (I Cor. 3:4-6).

What was the spiritual status of Apollos when he first came to Ephesus? From Luke's description, what Apollos knew was true as far as it went. He had accepted the ministry of John, which involved a readiness for the Messiah. He knew something of Jesus, but not the full significance of his life and teachings (18:25). His case seems similar to that of the twelve men whom Paul met (19:1-7). Although his knowledge was at first imperfect, when more light was presented to him he immediately accepted. "My sheep hear my voice" (John 10:27). Before the encounter with Aquila and Priscilla, it is best to regard Apollos in the same class as OT saints. They too hoped for salvation in Messiah and had not rejected him. The entire Book of Acts depicts the transition from Judaism to Christianity. It is not surprising, therefore, to find imperfect forms of faith during those epochal days.

II. THE VISIT TO EPHESUS (19:1-41)

A. *The Baptism of Twelve Disciples* (19:1-7)

Paul arrived in Ephesus by way of the upper country.[3] The statement in 19:1 is apparently a resume' of 18:23. Ramsay explains the expression as meaning the higher and more direct route to Ephesus, rather than the regular trade route through the Lycus and Maeander valleys.[4]

The disciples whom Paul met at Ephesus puzzle us as to their

---

[3]Greek: *ta anōterika merē.*
[4]*St. Paul the Traveller,* p. 265.

identity. They could hardly have been Christians in the full sense
of that term, inasmuch as they knew little or nothing of the work
of Christ, the bestowal of the Holy Spirit, or Christian baptism.
It is tempting to designate them as disciples of Apollos since both
were limited in their knowledge to John's baptism, but if that
were the case, it is inexplicable why Apollos did not enlighten
them after his own expanded knowledge from Aquila and Priscilla. Apparently these were a distinct group of Jews, existing
independent of Apollos or Aquila and Priscilla in the large
metropolis of Ephesus. Their spiritual status was that of OT
saints who now had to face the decision concerning the Messiah.

When Paul met these disciples, they were presented to him as
believers, but he apparently detected some deficiency in their
comprehension of Christian truth. He therefore asked whether
they had received the Holy Spirit inasmuch as they claimed to
have believed.[5] For Paul this was the acid test of true Christian
belief. The answer of these disciples should probably be understood as meaning their ignorance as to whether the Holy Spirit
had been given. The word "given" does not actually appear in
the Greek text, but neither does it occur in a similar statement
in John 7:39, and yet "given" is most properly inferred there
also. These disciples were adherents of John the Baptist's teaching, and he had spoken of Christ who would baptize with the
Holy Spirit (Luke 3:16). They could hardly have been ignorant
of the Spirit's existence. It was the fulfilment of his promised
bestowal of which they were unaware.

Upon learning that these disciples had experienced John's
baptism, Paul elaborated upon the key features of John's preaching which called for repentance from sin and faith in Jesus, the
Coming One. The reaction to this explanation was immediate
and favorable, and all twelve received Christian baptism, followed by Paul's imposition of hands upon them and the coming
of the Spirit. The signs of speaking in tongues and prophesying
accompanied their new experience. This is the only instance in
the NT where mention is made that those who had received
John's baptism also needed Christian baptism. Whether it should
be inferred in all instances (e.g., Apollos, the twelve at Pente-

---

[5]The aorist participle *pisteusantes* (having believed) denotes coincident
action here. Thus ASV translates "when ye believed."

cost) is disputed, although the fact of its being done at Ephesus would seem to argue that it was the regular practice and the silence of Scripture in the other instances certainly does not deny that it was done.

B. *The Progress of the Gospel* (19:8-20)

Paul's teaching ministry at Ephesus began in the synagogue. It was remarkable that Paul was able to return to the synagogue after being there on his previous journey (18:19). Usually the Christian converts were expelled very soon along with Paul. At Ephesus, however, his message at the first visit was well received, and Aquila and Priscilla continued attending the synagogue (18:26). Now Paul himself was able to resume his synagogue teaching for three months. Nevertheless, sufficient Jews eventually rejected the message, so that Paul took his Christian converts with him and secured the use of a lecture hall belonging to a man named Tyrannus. Codex Beza states that Paul used these quarters from the fifth to the tenth hour (11 A.M. to 4 P.M.), the period when most persons would be resting and the lecture hall would not be in use. During the next two years the Word of God was proclaimed through all of proconsular Asia, of which Ephesus was the capital. Probably at this time occurred the founding of the churches at Colosse, Hierapolis, and the seven cities of Revelation 2-3. A careful study of the Corinthian epistles reveals that during this period Paul also wrote several letters to Corinth, including the canonical First Corinthians (I Cor. 5:9; 16:8; II Cor. 2:4, 9; 7:8-12), and may have made a quick visit to that church (II Cor. 2:1).

The ministry at Ephesus was characterized also by numerous miracles including healings and exorcisms. Paul is not said to have recommended the use of cloths from his own body as instruments of healing, but God was pleased to honor the faith of these people by granting these miracles.

Demonic activity appeared prominently in opposition to Paul's ministry. Four such instances are mentioned in Acts, of which three were encountered by Paul (Bar-Jesus, Philippian girl, Sceva's sons). Seven itinerant exorcists adopted the name of the Lord as preached by Paul in order to increase their effectiveness. That Jews were sometimes involved in exorcism is

corroborated by the statement of Jesus (Matt. 12:27), as well
as by the many forms of the Divine Name found in formulas of
incantation among the papyri (*Iaō, Ia, Iaōia, Iaē, Aia,* and
Jaoth).[6] No Jewish high priest named Sceva is otherwise known
to us. The title may be used in the broad sense of a head of
one of the priestly families (as in 5:24). Jackson and Lake, however (and Bruce also), regard it as merely the claim or adver-
tisement of the exorcists.[7] Luke's sense of humor is evident here
as he describes the startling results experienced by the would-be
exorcists! It all contributed to the publicizing of the gospel. The
burning of the magic books shows the widespread effect of the
Christian message in Ephesus. The fame of the "Ephesian
Grammata" or magical writings was great,[8] and the burning of
50,000 drachmas' worth of them was a significant development.[9]

C. *The Plans of Paul* (19:21, 22)

It was while Paul was at Ephesus that he formed his plan to
visit Rome. The accomplishment would have to wait, however,
until he had made a tour of Macedonia and Achaia and had
gone to Jerusalem. The epistles reveal that one of his reasons for
going to Jerusalem was to deliver the collection from the churches
(I Cor. 16:1-3; also Acts 24:17). In the meantime Timothy and
Erastus were sent ahead to Macedonia. Timothy must also have
gone to Corinth (I Cor. 4:17).

It can be questioned whether Paul's own spirit or the Holy
Spirit is meant in 19:21. However, for the Christian the two
should be in harmony, and nothing here indicates that Paul
was planning contrary to the leading of the Lord.

D. *The Riot of the Silversmiths* (19:23-41)

The most dramatic episode during Paul's stay at Ephesus was
the riot provoked by Demetrius the silversmith. Ephesus was

---

[6]See Adolph Deissmann, *Bible Studies,* pp. 321-336.

[7]Jackson and Lake, *The Acts of the Apostles,* IV, 241; Bruce, *The Book
of the Acts,* p. 390.

[8]They are referred to by Clement of Alexandria in *The Stromata,* Book V,
Ch. 8.

[9]Suetonius mentions a similar burning of books of prophecy by Augustus
in Rome. "Augustus," XXI, *Twelve Caesars.*

Fig. 18. The theater at Ephesus, scene of the riot of the silversmiths. Seating capacity was approximately 25,000. Levant Photo Service

the headquarters of the worship of Artemis,[10] and her temple was one of the Seven Wonders of the ancient world. The image within the temple was of a woman carved with many breasts to signify the fertility of nature. It was reputed to be so ancient that the tradition arose that it had fallen from heaven (19:35). Perhaps it was originally made from a meteorite. Silversmiths in Ephesus had developed a lucrative business by selling small replicas of the shrine. Terra cotta ones have survived, although no silver ones have yet been found (they would have been melted down and re-used by later peoples because of their value).

By appealing to their economic losses and the threat to their religion posed by Paul's preaching, Demetrius agitated the citizenry, and a wild mob surged into the twenty-five thousand

[10]The KJV has used the Latin name Diana. The goddess was the Oriental deity of fertility, not the Greek goddess of the hunt who had the same name.

seat theater dragging with them two of Paul's associates, Gaius and Aristarchus.[11]

Paul wanted to go to the assistance of his friends, but the extreme danger caused his followers to restrain him. Some of the leading citizens, called Asiarchs, had become acquainted with Paul, and they also urged that he not take such a risk. "Asiarch" was the title given to representatives of the various cities in the province who were elected annually to preside over the "Rome and the Emperor" cult.[12]

The identity of Alexander is uncertain.[13] He may have been a Christian Jew (since Luke knew his name) who was pushed forward by the Jews in the crowd so that all the blame would fall on the Christians and not on the Jewish community which was also well known for its monotheism. Or he may have been a non-Christian Jew whose mission was to lay the blame on the Christians. Luke could have known his name because he later became a Christian. Whoever he was, the crowd refused to listen when they saw his Jewish appearance. Completely out of control, for two hours the crowd chanted in a frenzy.

The town clerk[14] finally got the attention of the people. He pointed out that the importance of Ephesus in relation to Artemis was known far and wide, and his implication was that a few men (Gaius and Aristarchus) could hardly change that. He further reminded them that due process of law should always be followed if there were legitimate complaints.[15] Otherwise Rome might very well launch an investigation into such displays of disorder.

---

[11]Although most manuscripts identify these men by the plural form "Macedonians," a very few use the singular, thus restricting it to Aristarchus. This would make it possible for Gaius to be the same person as Gaius of Derbe (20:4).

[12]See the extended Note XXII, "The Asiarchs" by Lily Ross Taylor in Jackson and Lake, *The Acts of the Apostles*, V, 256-262.

[13]There is no indication that he is to be identified with any of the other Alexanders in the NT.

[14]Greek: *grammateus*. This official was the executive officer who issued the decrees passed by the asembly.

[15]The mention of "proconsuls" (KJV "deputies," 19:38) is probably a generalizing plural, inasmuch as there was only one proconsul at a time in any province. The meaning is that there were such people in the empire as proconsuls who conducted courts.

III. THE TOUR THROUGH MACEDONIA, ACHAIA, AND TROAS (20:1-16)

A. *Macedonia* (20:1, 2)

Leaving Ephesus soon after the uproar at the theater, Paul went northward toward Macedonia. At Troas he had expected to meet Titus (II Cor. 2:12, 13), but did not until he reached Macedonia (II Cor. 7:5-7). It was following this reunion with Titus which brought good news from the troubled church at Corinth that Paul wrote Second Corinthians from Macedonia (II Cor. 8:1; 9:2-4).

B. *Achaia* (20:3-5)

After visiting the Macedonian churches (Philippi, Thessalonica, Berea), Paul came to Greece proper, usually designated by its provincial name of Achaia. Here he remained three months at Corinth, during which time he wrote the Epistle to the Romans. His host was Gaius (Titius Justus?) (Rom. 16:23; Acts 18:7). When Paul was ready to leave by ship for Syrian Antioch, a plot against him was discovered. Apparently the plan was to murder him at sea. Therefore, he changed his route to an overland trip back through Macedonia.

The list of Paul's companions is enumerated by their home regions. In all likelihood Luke has named for us the messengers designated by the various churches to carry the collection to Jerusalem. Sopater the son of Pyrrhus[16] was from Berea, and Aristarchus and Secundus were from Thessalonica. Philippi is not mentioned but may have been represented by Luke. Gaius was the delegate from Derbe, and Timothy was from Lystra (16:1). From the churches of Asia were Tychicus and Trophimus. No representatives are mentioned from Corinth, but their offering may have been sent previously by Titus and two other brethren (II Cor. 8:6-24). This group went on ahead and waited for Paul to join them at Troas.

C. *Troas* (20:6-16)

As the group left Philippi for Troas, the "we" narrative is re-

---

[16]This reading has the strong support of P[74] Aleph A B D E.

sumed. The most common assumption is that the author Luke rejoined the party at Philippi. The previous "we" section ended at Philippi on the Second Journey (16:40; 17:1). Luke had apparently remained there to oversee the new church. Paul and his group set sail after the close of the week-long feast of Unleavened Bread which followed immediately after Passover. He hoped to reach Jerusalem by Pentecost (20:16), and there was no time to waste.

Paul met with the Christians at Troas at their regular meeting time on the first day of the week. This appears to be Sunday night rather than Saturday night[17] inasmuch as Luke calls daybreak "on the morrow" ("the next day," NASB, 20:7). No explanation is given in Scripture as to why the early Christians changed their meeting day from Saturday to Sunday,[18] but the most likely reason is that they were commemorating the resurrection of Christ who arose on the first day of the week and met with the disciples that same day (Luke 24:1, 13, 33-36; John 20:1, 19). The observance of the Lord's Supper was a principal reason for the gathering. As was the custom in the early church, the partaking of the bread and cup seems here to have been combined with an agape or love feast. The word "eaten[19] (20:11) is used elsewhere in the NT of the satisfying of hunger (not just a sampling) and could easily denote the agape.

The restoration of Eutychus is described in terms of an actual raising from the dead. As this young man sat in the window slit of a room made increasingly stuffy by the crowd and the smoke of many oil lamps, he dozed off and fell three stories to the ground. When Dr. Luke says he was taken up dead, he says it differently from his description of Paul at Lystra ("supposing he had been dead," 14:19). Paul's statement about Eutychus, "his life is in him," was made after he had fallen upon him and embraced him. By this time the youth was again alive.

---

[17]If Jewish rather than Roman reckoning were used, the first day of the week began at sundown instead of at midnight, and thus Saturday night could technically be the first day of the week. But if so, daybreak would not be "the next day" but part of the same day.

[18]An even earlier instance of Sunday worship appears in I Cor. 16:2, written several months earlier while Paul was in Macedonia.

[19]Greek: *geusamenos*.

Paul did not sail with the others, but went by land to Assos. This would have enabled him to remain a bit longer at Troas (it was considerably shorter by land from Troas to Assos than by sea). At Assos he met the ship, and the group sailed to the city of Mitylene (on the island of Lesbos). The following days of sailing took them to Chios (an island), Samos[20] (an island), and then to the city of Miletus, thirty miles from Ephesus. Paul's desire to reach Jerusalem by Pentecost afforded him only fifty days from Passover, and already at least twenty-four of them had been used.[21] Thus he wisely desired to bypass Ephesus with its large church and many problems which would almost certainly produce delays.

IV. THE HOMEWARD JOURNEY (20:17–21:16)

A. *Farewell to the Ephesian Elders* (20:17-38)

Calling for the elders from the Ephesian church to meet him at Miletus, Paul addressed them with a most poignant message. These officials are called "overseers" (or bishops) in 20:28, showing that the titles were interchangeable at this time. He first reviewed his own ministry at Ephesus (20:18-21). It had been a faithful and wholehearted one with no cause for shame.

Paul next discussed his prospects for future ministry (20:22-27). He spoke of his present journey to Jerusalem, and the dangers about which he had been warned. It should be noted that the Spirit did not prohibit his going, but told him what would happen when he arrived.

The Ephesian elders were told that they would not all see his face again (20:25). Inasmuch as the Pastoral Epistles imply that Paul did return to Ephesus after his first Roman imprisonment, this passage may reflect either Paul's personal feelings of foreboding at this time, or else one may emphasize the "all" in 20:25, and understand that not all of these Ephesian elders

---

[20]KJV mentions Trogyllium, a coastal promontory which must have been encountered, and which appears in the Western and Byzantine texts. It is not mentioned, however, in P[74] Aleph A B C E.

[21]Seven days for Unleavened Bread (20:6), 12 days for the voyage and visit in Troas (20:6), 1 day each for voyages to Assos, Mitylene, Chios, Samos, and Miletus (20:13-15).

would be alive or at the same place, even if Paul should return at some future day.[22]

The final part of Paul's message concerned the responsibility of the Ephesian elders (20:28-35). Difficult days lay ahead with adversaries from within as well as from without the church. The responsibility of these overseers was the solemn one of caring for the church of God which had been acquired by the blood of God's own One.[23] Paul himself had engaged in this work for three years.[24] In so doing he had carefully avoided any appearance of monetary covetousness, and had exemplified the words of Jesus, "It is more blessed to give than to receive" (20:35). This saying is one of the *agrapha*, a term used to describe sayings of Jesus which are not recorded in the four gospels. That there were many such can hardly be doubted (John 21:25).

B. *Return to Palestine* (21:1-16)

1. *Tyre* (21:1-6)

After a tearful farewell at Miletus, Paul and his party took a coastal vessel which stopped at the islands of Cos and Rhodes before reaching the mainland port of Patara. There they transferred to a larger merchant ship which went across the open sea south of Cyprus until it reached the Phoenician city of Tyre in the province of Syria.

At Tyre the group made contact with the Christians and stayed with them seven days. Tyre had been evangelized following Stephen's death (11:19). It was here that the disciples urged Paul through the Spirit not to set foot in Jerusalem.

Did Paul disobey the Holy Spirit by going to Jerusalem? It must be remembered that Paul's ministry was characterized by a sensitivity to the Spirit's leading (16:6-10), which increases

---

[22]See Homer A. Kent, Jr., *The Pastoral Epistles* (Chicago, 1958), pp. 45, 46.

[23]F. F. Bruce shows how the expression *tou idiou* is equivalent here to "only" or "well-beloved" as a term of endearment, and is decidedly preferable to the KJV rendering. *The Acts of the Apostles*, p. 381.

[24]A round number including the two years (19:10) and three months (19:8) explicitly mentioned by Luke, plus some prior time (19:1-7) and perhaps some activity subsequent to his lecturing in the hall of Tyrannus (19:22).

the probability for right action here also. His reasons for going to Jerusalem were proper (20:16, 24; 24:11, 17). Furthermore, he was making this trip by the Spirit's constraint (19:21; 20:22). The Spirit had been revealing the dangers which awaited (20:23), but these were part of Paul's commission (9:16). Paul never gave any indication that he felt it was a mistake (23:1; 24:16). What happened in 21:4 was probably similar to the later instance in Caesarea with Agabus, where the information revealed by the Holy Spirit through the prophet was utilized by the people to urge Paul not to endanger himself (21:10-12). Paul, however, regarded it not as a prohibition but a divine forewarning so that he would be spiritually prepared for what would happen.

2. *Ptolemais* (21:7)

The distance from Tyre to Ptolemais is about twenty-seven miles. The present name of this city is Acre, and it is mentioned in the OT as Accho (Judg. 1:31). In Roman times it held the status of a colony because Claudius had settled a group of veterans in the city.

3. *Caesarea* (21:8-16)

This distance from Ptolemais to Caesarea was about forty miles. Whether the journey was made by sea or by land is not certain. Paul and his party stayed with Philip the evangelist (not the apostle), who has previously appeared in Acts as one of the Seven (6:5). He was last mentioned in Acts 8 where he had preached in Samaria and adjacent regions until he reached Caesarea. Apparently he had settled there, and now twenty to twenty-five years later appears in Caesarea with a family of four fine daughters. The historian Eusebius states that these daughters were informants regarding the early history of the church.[25] In those days before the completion of the NT canon, these daughters prophesied by conveying revelation from God. We may be confident that they did so in accord with the same spiritual principles explained by Paul (I Cor. 11:5; 14:34-35; I Tim. 2:11-12).

---

[25]Eusebius bases his information upon the report of Papias. *Ecclesiastical History,* Book III, Chapter 39.

Agabus[26] was mentioned in 11:28, where he predicted the famine. In making his prophecy of Paul's seizure in Jerusalem, he used the dramatic form of prediction quite common in the OT (see I Kings 11:29-39; Isa. 20:2-6; Jer. 13:1-11; Ezek. 4:1ff.). Agabus' prophecy conveyed information, not prohibition.[27] Although the believers (including Luke) responded with a most natural concern for Paul's safety, Paul himself could not be dissuaded from what he felt to be the will of God.

The mention of Mnason is made clearer in NASB. Apparently he was an early disciple who had quarters in Jerusalem sufficiently large to house the missionary party.[28] With the arrival in the city, the third missionary journey came to its close. For Paul the immediate future was uncertain, but the memories of a most fruitful tour must have brought satisfaction to the apostle's heart.

QUESTIONS FOR DISCUSSION

1. How do you explain the spiritual status of Apollos before he met Aquila and Priscilla?
2. Did Eutychus actually die when he fell from the window?
3. Did Paul disobey the Holy Spirit by going to Jerusalem?
4. Were the details of Agabus' prophecy literally fulfilled?
5. Why do Christians sometimes interpret the Spirit's will in opposite ways?

---

[26]In mentioning that Agabus came to Caesarea from Judea (21:10), Luke is using ethnic terminology and is regarding Caesarea as a gentile city, although it was actually the capital of Judea.

[27]The details of the prophecy would lead one to expect something slightly different from what eventually happened. In the prophecy the Jews would bind Paul (but in 21:33 it was the Romans who did it), and would deliver him to the gentiles (actually, the Romans took Paul away from the Jews). However, the main point is clear that Paul would be seized by the Jews and then fall into the hands of the gentiles. It is not inconceivable, however, that the Jews did bind him first (21:30), and their delivering of him to the Romans could be understood as forced rather than voluntary.

[28]It is possible, however, that Mnason's home was located on the route to Jerusalem, inasmuch as the distance to Jerusalem from Caesarea (60-70 miles) was too great for one day's travel.

Chapter 11

PAUL'S FINAL VISIT TO JERUSALEM
(Acts 21:17—23:35)

Did Paul arrive in time for Pentecost (20:16) as he hoped? Luke does not say, and the time would have been close, but there are hints from the multitudes in Jerusalem that he did (21:20, 27). As he reached Jerusalem after his long and eventful journey, one can scarcely imagine the feelings which almost must have overwhelmed him. He would be seeing friends of long standing, and would be delivering the gift of money that had been collected among the gentile churches during his tour. He could report on the many successes of his third missionary journey. He would have the special thrill of introducing to the Jerusalem Christians a number of his gentile converts who had been won during his ministry and now accompanied him to the city.

On the other hand Paul knew that his visit would not be one of uninterrupted triumph. The Holy Spirit had been warning him of the dangers to befall him. Agabus had specified in some detail that both Jew and gentile would lay hands on him with evil intent. Furthermore, Paul must have been aware that even the Christians were divided in their estimate of him, and some believers had seriously misunderstood his intentions and actions. Many conflicting currents were converging at Jerusalem, and needed only Paul's arrival to provide the crisis.

I. PAUL'S VISIT WITH JAMES AND THE ELDERS
(21:17-26)

The missionaries were warmly greeted by the believers in Jerusalem, and the second day Paul and his companions met with James[1] and the other officials of the church. They too praised God when they heard Paul's report of the spiritual victories among the gentiles during his just-completed tour.

---

[1]This was James the Lord's brother who emerges as the leader of the Jerusalem church after the departure of the apostles (12:17; 15:13).

They informed Paul, however, of a developing problem. Reports were circulating that he had been urging the Jews of the Diaspora[2] to abandon Mosaic traditions including circumcision. This was clearly untrue (remember the case of Timothy, 16:1-3), for Paul never derided his Jewish heritage nor demanded that Jewish Christians repudiate their Scriptures. (He did, of course, resist any attempt to force *gentiles* to comply with the Mosaic Law). James and the others feared that the presence of Paul in Jerusalem along with a vast throng of Jews attending the feast from all over the world would precipitate a problem.

It was suggested to Paul that he could put this slander to rest by showing publicly his respect for the Mosaic Law. Four men of their number had recently taken a Nazirite vow (see Num. 6:1-21). Such vows were usually taken for a period of thirty days. These men, however, had contracted some defilement, perhaps by touching a dead body, and could not complete the period of the vow until the seven-day rites of purification were performed. Paul could show his respect for Jewish customs by associating himself with these men and paying for their sacrifices.[3] The apostle agreed to the plan and the next day began his official association with the four men.

Paul has been criticized for this action, being viewed as compromising the very principle of freedom from the Law which he strongly espoused on other occasions.[4] It should be remembered however, that Paul's policy among Jews was one of expediency where the principle of grace was not at stake (16:2; I Cor. 9:19-20). Furthermore, the Jerusalem elders had not momentarily forgotten the decision of the Jerusalem Council, for they referred to it at this time (21:25). Historically this was still a period of transition, and thus we find the Jewish segment of the church still following temple worship and feasts (18:21; 20:16; 24:11). As long as it was voluntary and not imposed upon gentiles, Paul nowhere teaches that such activity was wrong for Jews.

---

[2]A term commonly used to denote Jews who lived away from Palestine.

[3]Such action was not without precedent. Agrippa I paid for many Nazirite sacrifices. Josephus, *Antiquities* XIX.6.1.

[4]So G. Campbell Morgan, *The Acts of the Apostles* (New York, 1924), p. 485.

II. PAUL'S ARREST AT THE TEMPLE (21:27–22:29)

A. *Paul Seized in the Temple* (21:27-40)

The seven days of purification were still in process when some Jews from Asia (non-Christians, of course) saw Paul in the temple, probably in the Court of Israel (i.e., Court of the Men). They were familiar with Paul from his long stay in Ephesus, and may also have known Trophimus. Remembering that they had seen Paul and Trophimus together in the city, they jumped to the conclusion that Paul had brought the gentile into the forbidden area of the temple.

Fig. 19. Barricade Inscription from Herod's Temple, announcing death to any Gentile who passed beyond the barrier. The Louvre

A low balustrade known as the Soreg separated the Court of the Gentiles from the inner courts to which only Jews were allowed. Signs in Greek and Latin were posted (of which two have been discovered) announcing the death penalty to any gentile found inside. The text is translated as follows:

No foreigner is to enter within the balustrade and enclosure around the temple area. Whoever is caught will have himself to blame for his death which will follow.

The Romans allowed the Jews the right to execute violators of this prohibition, even including Roman citizens.[5] In view of the suspicions already gathered around Paul (he was actually in the temple trying to allay those suspicions), it is absurd to suppose he would have taken Trophimus inside. (And even if he had, Trophimus would have been the one to die, and Paul would have been only an accessory.)

Seizing Paul in one of the inner courts, the Jews dragged him out to the Court of the Gentiles and set about beating him to death. Word reached the Roman chief captain (named Claudius

---

[5]Josephus quotes a statement to this effect from Titus. *Wars* VI.2.4.

Fig. 20. Model of the Fortress Antonia, where Paul spoke to the crowd from the stairs. Palphot Limited

Lysias, 23:26), and he came immediately to the scene of the riot with perhaps as many as two hundred soldiers[6] and took custody of Paul. Roman troops in Jerusalem were stationed at the fortress Antonia,[7] which adjoined the temple area at the northwest corner and afforded a view of its activities.

As Paul was being taken to the fortress, he asked permission to speak to the captain. This surprised the captain who had not expected to find a Greek-speaker in this disheveled prisoner. He had already guessed that he had captured the Egyptian guerilla leader who had escaped after a battle in which four hundred of his four thousand followers were slain by the Romans.[8] Paul however, identified himself as a Jew of Tarsus, thus accounting for his knowledge of Greek, and asked if he might attempt to pacify the crowd. Permission was granted, and from the elevation of the fortress stairs, he addressed the riotous Jews in the Aramaic language.[9]

B. *Paul's Speech on the Fortress Stairs* (22:1-21)

When Paul began his explanation, his use of Aramaic rather than the more cosmopolitan Greek took the crowd by surprise, and they gave him their attention. He first explained that he was a Jew, whose orthodox background was impeccable (22:1-5). Even though he was foreign born, he had been educated in Jerusalem under the celebrated Gamaliel. His zeal for Jewish traditions had been unquestioned, as his persecution of the Way attested.[10]

Paul next showed how it was that such a staunch Jew had become a convert to Jesus Christ (22:6-16). This is the second of three recitals of Paul's conversion in Acts (see 9:1-30), and

---

[6]There were at least two centurions, each of whom normally commanded 100 men.

[7]For a description of the fortress Antonia, see Josephus *Wars* V.5.8.

[8]Josephus *Wars* II.13.5; *Antiquities* XX.8.6. Josephus cites the figure of 30,000, but this may include all of his sympathizers, while 4,000 refers to his militia.

[9]It is generally conceded that references in the NT to "the Hebrew tongue" indicate Aramaic, except in Rev. 9:11 and 16:16.

[10]These were matters that could presumably be verified in Sanhedrin records.

the first to be related by Paul himself. The minor variations in details among the three accounts are not impossible to harmonize, and are the sort to be expected when verbal reports are given. The statement that Paul's companions did not hear the voice of the One speaking to Paul (22:9) seems to conflict with the earlier notice that they heard the voice but saw no one (9:7). It may be significant that the verb "to hear"[11] uses different grammatical cases for its objects in these two instances. Perhaps in 9:7 the use of the genitive case implies that they heard a sound coming from some unidentified source, whereas the accusative case in 22:9 indicates that they did not hear it as intelligible speech. Another possibility is that the companions heard only the voice of Paul, but not the voice of the One who addressed him.

When he was led into Damascus, the devout Jew Ananias was used by God to restore Paul's sight and convey God's message. A literal translation of Ananias' closing words is as follows: "Arise, get yourself baptized[12] and your sins washed away, having called[13] on His name" (22:16). Both imperatives are in light of the fact that Paul had already called upon the name of the Lord. Inasmuch as calling upon the name of the Lord brings salvation (Rom. 10:13), water baptism must be an act of obedience subsequent to salvation. Baptism symbolized the method of salvation (identification with Christ) and washing symbolized the result (cleansing from sin).

The final portion of Paul's speech explained how he became the apostle to the gentiles (22:17-21). Even as a Christian he still worshipped in the temple when he was at Jerusalem. On one such occasion he was instructed by the Lord to leave the city. When he had remonstrated by insisting that his background as a persecutor would grant him an audience with the Jews, no less a personage than the Lord himself ordered Paul to leave with the words, "I will send you far away to the gentiles." Paul had not repudiated his people. He had preached to gentiles only because God had directly ordered it.

---

[11]Greek: *akouō*.

[12]Both *baptisai* and *apolousai* are midle voice aorists.

[13]Greek: *epikalesamenos* (aorist middle participle).

C. *The Response of the Jews and the Romans* (22:22-29)

The "word"[14] which ignited the fury of the Jews was the name "gentiles" in 22:21. Even though Paul was quoting the actual statement of Jehovah in the temple, the suggestion of gentile equality in matters of salvation was abhorrent to their traditions. Jews believed in proselytizing gentiles, but not apart from requiring submission to the Mosaic Law. The crowd reacted in a characteristic mode of Oriental displeasure, casting off their robes and throwing handfuls of dirt into the air.

The Roman captain apparently did not understand Aramaic, and thus had no real knowledge of the point at issue. He therefore planned to uncover the truth by a time-honored method of law-enforcement officers — torture of the prisoner. If this scourging denoted use of the Roman *flagellum*, it was far more serious than a beating with rods (16:23), or even than the lash employed by Jewish authorities (5:40). The whip was imbedded with pieces of metal or bone, and was capable of bringing death or at least permanent crippling.

Because it was illegal to apply the scourge to Roman citizens, especially when they had not even been tried, Paul claimed his Roman citizenship to escape needless suffering.[15] Claudius Lysias was amazed, particularly since it turned out that Paul's citizenship had been acquired by birth,[16] whereas Lysias had purchased his. It is not known whether a citizen carried papers to prove his citizenship, but to claim it falsely was a most serious offense. Suetonius relates regarding Rome that any who usurped the rights of Roman citizens were executed on the slopes of the Esquiline Hill.[17] The captain immediately desisted from any further attempts to scourge him, and even though he had not actually done it, he was fearful lest his preparations to do so upon a Roman citizen might be used in some way to his discredit.

---

[14]The Greek term *logos,* however, may also mean "statement."

[15]This feature makes it clear that Claudius Lysias must have understood Paul's previous claim of being "a citizen of no mean city" to refer to Tarsus, not to Rome (21:39).

[16]How Paul's father became a Roman citizen is not known. Perhaps it was because of some special service to the empire.

[17]Suetonius, "Claudius," XXV, *The Twelve Caesars.*

III. PAUL BEFORE THE SANHEDRIN (22:30–23:11)

A. *The Sanhedrin Meeting* (22:30–23:10)

On the day following Paul's arrest, the captain arranged this meeting of the Sanhedrin to ascertain the charge against Paul. This was at least the fifth time that the Sanhedrin had to evaluate the Christian movement.[18] Paul began his statement by remarking that he was no opponent of OT religion, for he had lived in good conscience before God right down to the present.[19] This provoked the outrageous command from the high priest Ananias that Paul be slapped on the mouth for a supposedly blasphemous utterance. Paul's spirited response, "God shall smite you, you whitewashed wall!" is understandable, even though it may have been out of order (of course, Ananias' command was also out of order). Jesus had called the Pharisees "whitewashed tombs" (Matt. 23:27), and the Sadducees (to whom Ananias belonged) were certainly no better.

What did Paul mean by his statement, "I knew not, brethren, that he was the high priest"? It has been suggested that the high priest was not presiding at this meeting called by the Roman captain, and thus Paul did not realize who had issued the order. Others have suggested that Paul had poor eyesight. A more likely explanation is that Paul meant he did not recognize in Ananias the conduct of a high priest ("By his actions I would not have known he was high priest"). Perhaps the best answer is to see in these words an apology by Paul. The word "knew" is sometimes used in the sense of "acknowledge,"[20] and thus Paul may have meant that his retort did not acknowledge the dignity of the high priest's office. He admitted his error and quoted Exodus 22:28 to show his loyalty to the Law.

In spite of an inauspicious beginning, Paul still had hopes of getting some sort of intelligent hearing for his defense. Although

---

[18](1) Jesus' trial, (2) Peter and John (4:5ff.), (3) the Twelve (5:21ff.), (4) Stephen (6:12ff.), (5) Paul.

[19]He was not, of course, claiming sinlessness, nor was he referring to the inner spiritual conflicts of Rom. 7. The reference was to the externals of his life, and the blamelessness of his conduct as measured by the demands of the Law (cf. Phil. 3:4-6).

[20]This verb (*oida*) is so used in I Thess. 5:12, where it obviously means "acknowledge the position of," rather than "be acquainted with."

the high priest and many of the other Sanhedrin members were Sadducees, whose basic theological beliefs rejected such concepts as resurrection, angels, and other spirit beings (and thus they would deny the validity of his claim that Jesus was resurrected and had spoken to him, 22:8), Paul realized that there were also Pharisees present. At least he had reason to hope that they would understand. Unfortunately for his purposes, the two groups began haggling between themselves, and the argument became sufficiently violent that Paul's safety was once again in jeopardy. The resultant clamor required Lysias to rescue him and remove him to the fortress. One wonders what this pagan soldier must have thought of the religion of the Jews after witnessing such an exhibition.

B. *The Divine Appearance* (23:11)

Paul may well have been greatly discouraged at the way events were going in Jerusalem. Not only had his sincere attempt in the temple to show his respect for Jewish institutions resulted in a riot, but his effort to explain the situation to the Sanhedrin had fared no better. That night, however, the Lord appeared to Paul and commended him for his testimony in Jerusalem. Luke mentions five special appearances of the Lord to Paul at critical periods of his life.[21] There is nothing here to warrant the idea that Paul was out of the will of God by going to Jerusalem. Some have seen in the comparative statement "as . . . so . . ." an indication that the Lord was revealing to Paul that he would testify in Rome as a prisoner, just as he had in Jerusalem, thus informing him not only of the fact but also of the manner.

IV. PAUL'S REMOVAL TO CAESAREA (23:12-35)

A. *The Conspiracy* (23:12-22)

The day following the explosive Sanhedrin meeting, forty Jews plotted to assassinate Paul, and took an oath calling upon God to smite them if they failed and vowing not to eat until the deed was done. They needed the complicity of the San-

---

[21]Damascus Road (9:4), two occasions in Jerusalem (22:17; 23:11), Corinth (18:9, 10), and the voyage to Rome (an angel, 27:23, 24).

hedrin to get Paul out in the open from Roman custody. Evidently the conspirators knew how morally rotten their leaders were, or they would not have suggested such a scheme to them. No wonder Paul later appealed to Caesar rather than appear before the Sanhedrin again (25:11).

Somehow Paul's nephew heard of the plot and informed Paul in the fortress.[22] We know practically nothing else of Paul's family (except that his father was a Roman citizen, 22:28). Whether the sister and her son lived in Jerusalem, or were just visiting, or whether the lad was studying there as Paul had done before him, must remain unanswered questions. It is commonly assumed that Paul's family disinherited him when he became a Christian. However, it must be noted that when Paul fled from the plot in Jerusalem after his conversion, he did go home to Tarsus (9:30). Furthermore, Paul's reference to his "kinsmen" who were "in Christ before me" (Rom. 7:16), although commonly interpreted "fellow-countrymen," employs a word that often meant "relatives." The whole matter is obscure but tantalizing.

When the captain heard the lad's story, he immediately recognized the danger, and cautioned the youth to say nothing about the report. He hoped to gain sufficient time to counteract this plot before the conspirators knew they had been discovered.

B. *The Night Journey to Caesarea* (23:23-35).

The captain Lysias ordered two hundred soldiers, seventy horsemen, and two hundred spearmen to be ready to leave Jerusalem for Caesarea at 9 p.m. Apparently he was taking no chances with the safety of his prisoner whose Roman citizenship had already posed certain difficulties. Frequent assassinations made him understandably cautious. He also wrote a letter of explanation to the procurator Felix. It will be obvious to the reader that Lysias was somewhat lax in his handling of the truth about how and when he learned of Paul's citizenship. The contents of this letter were probably told to Luke by Paul who

---

[22]A possible explanation of how Paul's nephew learned of the plot may be found in 23:16. The aorist participle *paragenomenos* (KJV "went") may be translated "having been present," and could denote the young man's presence at the plotters' meeting.

doubtless heard it read to Felix when he and the soldiers arrived.

Arriving in Antipatris after a forced march of approximately forty miles through the night, the foot soldiers returned to Jerusalem (the danger of ambush was now past), and the horsemen conducted Paul the rest of the way to Caesarea (another 25 miles or so). When the letter was read to the procurator Felix, he asked where Paul was from. He needed to be sure that he did not come from one of the petty kingdoms whose quasi-sovereignty needed to be respected. Learning that he was from a province (Cilicia), he agreed to hear the case. Meanwhile, the prisoner was to be kept in Herod's one-time palace, which was currently being utilized as the procurator's residence.

Antonius Felix was the brother of Pallas, the freedman who was a favorite of Claudius. He was appointed procurator of Judea in A.D. 52, but had served before that in Samaria at the time of Cumanus.[23] Both officially and personally, Felix was noted for his evil deeds. ". . . Antonius Felix, indulging in every kind of barbarity and lust, exercised the power of a king in the spirit of a slave."[24] With such a judge to hear the case, the results were most uncertain. But for the moment, Paul was safe from his enemies, and he had learned by direct revelation (23:11) that the Lord had not abandoned him.

QUESTIONS FOR DISCUSSION

1. How could Paul join the men with a Jewish vow if he believed that Christians are free from the Mosaic Law?
2. Did Paul take Trophimus inside the temple?
3. What did Paul mean by his statement before the Sanhedrin that he did not know it was the high priest whom he had insulted?
4. Does 22:16 teach that one must be baptized to be saved?
5. Why did Paul state to the Sanhedrin that he was a Pharisee?

---

[23]Tacitus *The Annals* XII, 54, in *Great Books of the Western World* (Chicago, 1952), Vol. 15.
[24]Tacitus *The Histories* V, 9.

Chapter 12

FELIX, FESTUS, AND AGRIPPA
(Acts 24-26)

The delivery of the prisoner Paul to Caesarea marked the beginning of a two-year imprisonment in that city. During this period he stated his case, and also the case for the Christian gospel, to two provincial governors and a king, fulfilling one aspect of the Lord's prediction about his ministry (9:15). While these were days of high drama, they were also times of long confinement allowing opportunity for reflection, planning, and perhaps for writing. Through it all Paul maintained his unswerving purpose, and grasped every opportunity to testify of God's remarkable working in his life and of the need for all men, both high and low, to respond in faith to the gospel of Christ.

I. PAUL BEFORE FELIX (24:1-27)

A. *The Accusation* (24:1-9)

Considering the distance from Jerusalem to Caesarea, five days was a very short time for the Sanhedrin to secure their lawyer, prepare their case, and travel to Caesarea. Perhaps they feared that if they did not come quickly, Paul might be released for lack of evidence.

The Jews had secured the services of a lawyer named Tertullus (probably a Jew with a Roman name). He began his speech to Felix by the customary flattering of the judge. He may have been put to considerable effort to find instances about which to praise Felix. Tacitus said of him that he "thought that he could do any evil act with impunity . . . ,"[1] and that he indulged "in every kind of barbarity and lust."[2] Later he was guilty of having the high priest Jonathan assassinated.[3] In spite of this wickedness, Tertullus was able to observe that "much peace"

---

[1]*Annals* XII, 54.
[2]*Histories* V, 9.
[3]Josephus *Antiquities* XX.8.5.

and certain "reforms" (24:3, NASB) had been accomplished by
Felix. He had put down numerous insurrections, had captured a
guerilla leader named Eleazar, and had driven away the Egyptian leader (with whom Lysias had mistakenly identified Paul.)[4]

The actual charges made against Paul were three. (1)
Treason. Paul was accused of disturbing the peace and creating

Fig. 21. Ruins of Caesarea, the Roman capital of Judea in New Testament times. Photo by the author

political dissension not only in Jerusalem but throughout the
world. (2) *Religious heresy.* By calling him a "ringleader of the
sect of the Nazarenes," the implication was that the Law of
Moses was being violated. (3) *Temple desecration.* The original
cry that Paul had taken a gentile into the temple (21:28) was
now softened to the charge that he tried to do so.

Some ancient manuscripts omit the words which appear in the

---

[4]Josephus *Antiquities* XX.8.5; *Wars* II.13.5.

KJV as verses 6b-8a.[5] If the omission is sustained, then verse 8b refers to Felix' examination of Paul (so NASB). If the words in question are genuine, verse 8b refers to Felix' questioning of Lysias. Assuming for the moment that the words belong in the text, it is obvious that Tertullus has been even more highhanded with the truth than Claudius Lysias was (23-27), for the Jews had not seized Paul so as to judge him by the Mosaic Law, but were about to beat him to death until he was rescued by the Romans.

B. *Paul's Defense* (24:10-21)

Paul's defense was built around answering the three charges (the same three charges are mentioned again in 25:8, as in 21:28 and 24:5, 6). He avoided hollow flattery of Felix, but courteously acknowledged the many years of his tenure,[6] a fact which would make the procurator more capable of understanding Paul's argument.

Paul first answers the charge of treason by stating that he had not been in Jerusalem long enough to stir up all the insurrection of which he was accused (24:11-13). Only twelve days ago had he arrived in the city, and for five of those he had been in custody. He had gathered no crowds about him. As far as causing sedition throughout the world, no witnesses or other proofs were offered.

The chronology involved in the "twelve days" poses problems inasmuch as the five days in Caesarea (24:1) added to the seven days of purification (21:27) exhaust the total without including other events Luke has described. A number of explanations are possible, as the following examples indicate:

Day 1	Arrival in Jerusalem
Day 2	Meeting with James
Days 3-7	Days of purification

---

[5]The omission involves the words "and would have judged . . . commanding his accusers to come unto thee." The material appears in the Western and Byzantine texts but is omitted by P[74] Aleph A B P. There is considerable doubt among scholars about the omission, and many feel that the words in question may be original.

[6]Felix had been procurator since A.D. 52 (it was now A.D. 56), and before that he had served in Samaria under his predecessor Cumanus (Tacitus *Annals* XII, 54).

Day 8	Before Sanhedrin
Day 9	Conspiracy reported to Lysias
Day 10	Arrival in Caesarea
Days 11, 12	In Caesarea
Day 13	Before Felix

This procedure includes five days of the seven-day purification, thus allowing for their being "almost" completed (21:27). It also computes the five days of 24:1 from the time Paul left Jerusalem, not from his arrival in Caesarea, and does not count the appearance before Felix as one of the twelve days.

Another scheme reconstructs the chronology this way:

Day 1	Arrival in Jerusalem
Day 2	Meeting with James
Days 3-5	Days of purification
Day 6	Before Sanhedrin
Day 7	Conspiracy reported to Lysias
Days 8-12	In Caesarea

This explanation allows only three days for the purification (which is hardly "almost" 7), and must suppose that Paul had joined the four men in the midst of their week.

Paul deals next with the charge of religious heresy (24:14-16). He admitted belonging to the Way, but went on to show that this did not make him apostate for he continued to serve the God of his fathers, he believed the OT Scriptures, and he continued to hold the orthodox Jewish hope of resurrection. Actually, Paul was more orthodox than the Sadducees among his accusers, for they had rejected the traditional Jewish belief in resurrection. Perhaps there were some Pharisees present in this delegation to whom he refers as believing in the resurrection. The resurrection of both righteous and wicked was clearly taught in such OT passages as Daniel 12:2.[7]

The final portion of Paul's defense answered the charge of temple desecration (24:17-21). He explained that he had recently been in Jerusalem after an absence of several years.[8]

---

[7]This, of course, does not infer that either the OT or Paul taught a general resurrection of all men simultaneously.

[8]His last visit had been 4 years before in A.D. 52 at the end of the second missionary journey (18:22).

He had come to bring offerings to his nation.[9] He denied any illegal activity in the temple, and noted that not one of the original accusers was even present to act as a witness. Even the Sanhedrin in Jerusalem had been unable to demonstrate any grounds for a trial. The only matter that had upset them was Paul's mention of resurrection, and this was hardly a crime (23:6).

C. *The Two-Year Detention* (24:22-27)

Felix had no desire to offend the official Jewish delegation from Jerusalem, so he postponed final disposition of the case pending the arrival of Lysias.[10] Paul was retained in custody but allowed to have visits from his friends.

The procurator Felix had some previous knowledge of the Way, perhaps because of his Jewish wife Drusilla. She was a daughter of Herod Agrippa I (the murderer of James, 12:1, 2), and the sister of Agrippa II and Bernice (25:13). Previously she had been married to Azizus, king of Emesa, but had left him to marry Felix. During Paul's imprisonment, Felix sent for him on numerous occasions, and with Drusilla heard him speak on the themes of righteousness, self-control, and judgment to come. The immoral lives of Felix and Drusilla left much opportunity for such truths to be applied.

Although Paul's words brought the terror of conviction to Felix, there was no repentance. He sent for Paul often, but it was partly in hopes of receiving a bribe for his release. This was a common practice among procurators, as Josephus records concerning Albinus, the successor of Festus.[11]

After two years there was a riot of pagans and Jews in Caesarea. The soldiers of Felix put it down with such violence that the outraged Jews were able to force his recall in A.D. 58.[12] Hoping to placate his Jewish accusers somewhat, he left Paul in prison for his successor Porcius Festus to deal with.

---

[9]This is the only mention in Acts of the collection for the saints.

[10]Luke does not state whether Lysias ever came. If he did, apparently he added nothing to the case which could hasten its settlement.

[11]*Wars* II.14.1.

[12]Josephus *Antiquities* XX.8.7,9.

II. PAUL BEFORE FESTUS (25:1-12)

A. *The Visit of Festus to Jerusalem* (25:1-5)

Porcius Festus succeeded Felix as governor of Judea in A.D. 58.[13] According to Josephus, he was a marked improvement over Felix, and was better than his successor Albinus.[14] Festus died after about two years in office.[15] When he assumed the governorship and arrived in the capital at Caesarea, he immediately undertook a trip to Jerusalem, the ancient capital of Judea and center of Jewish religious life. It was most important for a Roman procurator of Judea to establish some sort of working arrangement with the high priest and Sanhedrin if he were to govern with any degree of success. This was especially necessary following the unpleasantness between the Jews and Felix.

While Festus was in Jerusalem, the Jewish leaders informed the new procurator about Paul, and exerted considerable pressure to have Paul executed (25:15, 16). When this failed, they urged that Paul be brought to Jerusalem ostensibly for a trial, but actually that they might ambush him along the way. The Jews doubtless hoped to exploit the inexperience of Festus in Judea, knowing that he would be unaware of the previous plot which had necessitated Paul's removal to Caesarea. Festus, however, refused to allow this Jewish pressure to prevail, and countered with the proposal to hold a hearing in Caesarea. He promised to care for the matter speedily, provided that the Jews would send qualified persons to state the case against Paul.

B. *Paul's Defense* (25:6-12)

After concluding his brief visit of no more than eight or ten days,[16] Festus returned to his capital at Caesarea and held court for Paul's case the very next day. The Jewish representatives presented the same charges against Paul as they had done before (24:5, 6). No proof was offered; no witnesses took the

---

[13]This date is somewhat tentative, and others suggest dates ranging from A.D. 55 to 59.

[14]*Wars* II.14.1.

[15]Josephus *Antiquities* XX.9.1.

[16]The NASB or similar translations should be followed at 25:6, rather than KJV. The implication of the passage is that Festus rather quickly left Jerusalem, not that he delayed his return.

stand. Therefore, Paul simply made a categorical denial of each charge. He had not violated Jewish law, nor desecrated the temple, nor committed treason against Caesar.

Festus, however, was attempting to begin his governorship on a happy note with the Jews. He hoped that he could accede to their wishes (25:3), at least to the extent of transferring Paul to Jerusalem for another trial. Festus would be in charge ("before me," 25:9), and this should afford some protection to Paul's interests. But Paul did not consider this a reasonable prospect at all. He knew much better than Festus the attitude of the Sanhedrin. He knew how they had connived with the plotters to assassinate him. He could expect no justice in Jerusalem, and

Fig. 22. Nero, the Roman Caesar (A.D. 54-68) to whom Paul appealed. Fratelli Alinari

the possibility always existed that Festus might yield to the political pressures of the Sanhedrin. Because Paul was a Roman citizen and was presently before a Roman tribunal, there was no good reason for any kind of change. Yet it was now obvious that Festus was willing to accede to the Sanhedrin's desires. Therefore, Paul took the bold step of appealing his case to Caesar.

The appeal to Caesar was the right of a citizen to appeal the verdict of a magistrate. The right was supported by two technical processes, the *provocatio* and the *appellatio*.[17] Although originating as two separate procedures with somewhat different purposes, by the time of the Caesars both were combined and the appeal was to the emperor himself. When this appeal was allowed, all further proceedings in lower courts ceased, and the prisoner was sent to Rome for disposition of his case. Festus immediately conferred with his advisors, and when it was agreed that the appeal was valid, the procurator announced the fact to Paul and the others.

Paul has been accused of acting faithlessly in appealing to Caesar rather than trusting God. Nevertheless his use of the privileges allowed him by his government was consistent with the principles enunciated in Romans 13:1-4. Paul had spent two years in confinement with much opportunity to pray and reflect over possible courses of action. Today's readers are hardly in any position to criticize Paul's decision.

The Caesar to whom Paul appealed was Nero, who had begun his reign in A.D. 54. His early years of rule gave no hint of the cruelties that would follow. Suetonius wrote:

> Nero started off with a parade of virtue; giving Claudius a lavish funeral . . . .[18]
>
> As a further guarantee of his virtuous intentions, he promised to model his rule on the principles laid down by Augustus, and never missed an opportunity of being generous or merciful, or of showing what a good companion he was.[19]

---

[17]A thorough discussion is found in Jackson and Lake, *The Acts of the Apostles*, V, 312-319.

[18]"Nero," IX, *Twelve Caesars*.

[19]*Ibid.*, X.

III. PAUL BEFORE AGRIPPA (25:13–26:32)

A. *The Visit of Agrippa and Bernice* (25:13-27)

Not long after Festus assumed office, King Agrippa II and Bernice came to Caesarea to pay their respects to the new procurator. Agrippa was the son of Herod Agrippa I (12:1). When his father died in A.D. 44 (12:23), Agrippa was only seventeen, and was regarded as too young to assume his father's reign. Later Claudius gave him the territory of his uncle Herod king of Chalcis (at his death), which also carried with it the right of appointing the Jewish high priest and the custody of the high priest's garments which were used on the Day of Atonement. Thus he was the titular head of Jewish religion. A few years after, his territory was exchanged for Batanea, Gaulanitis, Trachonitis, and Abilene, and still later other areas were added by Nero.[20] His capital was Caesarea Philippi, northeast of the Sea of Galilee. Agrippa changed its name to Neronias in honor of Nero.

Bernice was the daughter of Herod Agrippa I, and sister of Drusilla and Agrippa II. She had been married to her uncle Herod king of Chalcis, and since his death she had been living with her brother Agrippa in a relationship that was widely rumored to be incestuous. She also married Polemon king of Cilicia, but deserted him. Later she became the mistress of both Vespasian and Titus, and lived in Rome.[21]

It should not be supposed that Festus was a subordinate to Agrippa. This visit was not that of a monarch to one of his underlings, but a courtesy call from a neighboring ruler to the new procurator of an adjoining province. During the course of the visit, Festus took the occasion to mention Paul's case to Agrippa. In his explanation he showed how little he really understood of Jewish affairs and of the Christian movement (unlike his predecessor Felix, 24:22). When Agrippa expressed an interest in hearing Paul (being partly Jewish, he doubtless had heard of him), Festus arranged a glittering state function

---

[20]Josephus, *Wars* II.12.1,8; *Antiquities* XIX.9.2; XX.1.1-3; XX.5.2; XX.7.1.

[21]Josephus *Wars* II.11.6; *Antiquities* XIX.9.1; XX.7.3; Suetonius, "Titus," VII, *Twelve Caesars;* Tacitus *Histories* II.2,81.

and brought Paul before his royal visitors along with other socially prominent dignitaries who had been assembled for the occasion. In addition to providing entertainment for his guests, it was the procurator's hope that this event might provide him with a clearer understanding of his puzzling prisoner, for he faced the embarrassment of sending a prisoner to the emperor without really knowing why it was necessary.

B. *Paul's Defense* (26:1-23)

Paul was not now on trial. All trials in the provincial courts had ceased the moment his appeal to the emperor was allowed. This occasion was arranged to satisfy Agrippa's interest in Paul, and also to provide Festus with information with which to write an accusation to send to Rome. Presumably as a citizen having appealed to Rome, Paul could have refused this interview, but he seized the opportunity to proclaim the gospel.

The apostle's introductory words were tactful and polite (26:1-3). He was also truthful as he expressed his gratitude for the opportunity to present his case before one who was knowledgeable about Judaism and could understand the real nature of his difficulties with the Jews. In contrast Festus was almost totally ignorant of Jewish religious teaching, and the subleties of the issues swirling around Paul were incomprehensible to him (25:18, 19; 26:24).

Paul first explained his past life as a Pharisee (26:4-11). He had been reared in the tenets of the most exacting and orthodox of the Jewish parties — the Pharisees. And it was one of the most basic beliefs of Judaism that lay at the heart of the accusations against him. Yet he was not a rejector but an exponent of that belief, for the issue was the hope of salvation for Israel. This had been promised to the patriarchs and enlarged by the prophets to include the sending of a divine Deliverer whose coming would bring the salvation for which they longed, and would also issue in resurrection that even those who had died might participate in Messiah's reign. Inasmuch as all Israel[22] believed in resurrection, the Christian proclamation of Jesus' resurrection should hardly be thought incredible, at least among

---

[22]The mention of "twelve tribes" (26:7) shows that Paul did not believe ten tribes have been lost (see also James 1:1).

Jews. Yet Paul himself had formerly misunderstood and had persecuted believers, imprisoning, voting for their deaths,[23] and trying to coerce them to renounce Christ through blasphemy.[24]

He then explained the radical change in his conversion (26:12-18). It took an arrest by God himself to change the course in which he was going. The supernatural experience on the Damascus Road confronted him with the Lord who identified himself as Jesus. This Jesus, who was now resurrected and in heaven, had commissioned him to proclaim forgiveness of sins through faith in the risen Lord.

Paul next discussed his subsequent life as a Christian (26:19-23). To one whose whole life had been characterized by devotion to the God of Israel, his present obedience to the vision was to be expected. It was his dedication to the message of Christ, based upon OT Scripture, that had caused the trouble in the temple at Jerusalem. Yet the OT itself foretold Messiah's suffering and resurrection, and this was the heart of the message Paul was proclaiming.

C. *The Reactions of Festus and Agrippa* (25:24-32)

For Festus there was little in Paul's speech that interested him. Discussion of Jewish Scriptures, vision, resurrection, and salvation for Jew and gentile, found in him no sympathetic response. Certainly the message contained little that would help Festus in writing his report to the emperor. His interjection, "Paul, you are mad!"[25] is not to be taken literally (Festus would not send a mental incompetent to Rome), but was Festus' observation that Paul's obvious learning must have unbalanced him.

With Agrippa, however, the situation was different and Paul knew this. Agrippa gave his official support to Judaism, and posed as a defender of its institutions. Paul had just shown that his ministry was in full accord with the teaching of the Scrip-

---

[23]Acts records no other deaths besides Stephen's to which this might refer, but there is no reason why we may not infer that others were killed during the persecutions (see 9:1; 22:4). This mention of Paul's vote is one of the chief evidences used to indicate his former membership in the Sanhedrin.

[24]An instance of the conative use of the imperfect tense *ēnankazon*. Hence "tried to cause them to blaspheme." Whether he was successful is not stated.

[25]Greek: *Mainēi, Paule.*

tures. He felt sure that Agrippa would acknowledge the validity of his arguments. The king, however, was not about to be maneuvered into an embarrassing corner. He said to Paul, "In a little, you are persuading to make me a Christian."[26] Of course, he did not mean that he was on the verge of becoming a convert (*en oligōi* does not mean "almost"). Rather, he meant that Paul's personal question (26:27) implied that with this one little interview he was actually trying to make a Christian out of Agrippa. To the king the thought must have seemed amusing. Paul, however, replied in all seriousness that both with this little amount of time and with much more time and effort if need be he wished that Agrippa and all the others would join him in his faith in Christ.

The interview was becoming too personal for his comfort so Agrippa ended it by rising along with Festus, Bernice, and the others. The innocence of Paul was readily admitted by these officials, and Agrippa indicated that only the pending appeal to Caesar prevented Paul's release. It should not be concluded that Paul had acted unwisely. If he had not appealed to Caesar, this interview would never have been held, for he would have been taken back to Jerusalem and ambushed along the way (25:3). Now there was but one way to go and that was to Rome.

QUESTIONS FOR DISCUSSION

1. What were the Jews' charges against Paul? Were any of them valid?
2. How did Felix really feel about Paul's message?
3. Should Paul have appealed to Caesar?
4. What were the main points which Paul explained before Agrippa?
5. Did Agrippa almost become a Christian?

---

[26]Greek: *En oligōi me peitheis Christianon poiēsai.*

Chapter 13

ROME AT LAST!
(Acts 27, 28)

Ever since the purpose of going to Rome had been planted in Paul's mind by the Holy Spirit, his plans had been formulated, with that goal in view (19:21). No warnings of dangers to come could make him deviate from that ultimate aim, nor from the intermediate stages (Macedonia, Achaia, Jerusalem). The intervening weeks had stretched into months and then into years, and Paul had been confronted with one crisis after another, but he had divine assurance that Rome would yet be reached (23:11). The means were not what Paul could have foreseen nor what he might have chosen, but God was in control and the apostle was fully willing to leave the details in His hands.

I. THE SEA VOYAGE (27:1-44)

A. *The Start of the Voyage* (27:1-8)

Paul and certain other prisoners[1] were placed in the charge of Julius, a centurion attached to the Augustan Cohort.[2] There is corroborating evidence for an Augustan Cohort in Syria during the first century.[3] Being unable to locate at Caesarea a ship going to Italy, the centurion secured passage for his prisoners on a ship of Adramyttium which would sail northward and then west along the southern coast of Asia (see Fig. 23). At some port in Asia he was certain to locate a larger vessel which was going to Rome.

Aristarchus and Luke ("we") accompanied Paul. Perhaps Aristarchus went merely as a passenger on his way home to Thessalonica. On the other hand, he was present with Paul in

---

[1]The use of *heterous* for these "other" prisoners may suggest that they were in a different category. Perhaps only Paul had appealed to Caesar, whereas the others were already sentenced to death.

[2]We have already encountered the Italian Cohort in 10:1.

[3]See the discussion in Jackson and Lake, *The Acts of the Apostles*, V, 427-445.

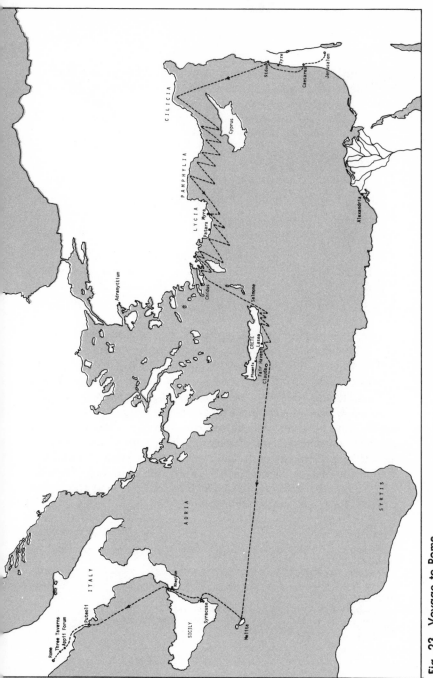

Fig. 23. Voyage to Rome

Rome, at least part of the time (Col. 4:10; Philem. 24). Ramsay suggested that both Luke and Aristarchus went as slaves of Paul.

> . . . In this way not merely had Paul faithful friends always beside him; his importance in the eyes of the centurion was much enhanced, and that was of great importance. The narrative clearly implies that Paul enjoyed much respect during this voyage, such as a penniless traveler without a servant to attend on him would never receive either in the first century or the nineteenth.[4]

The vessel proceeded northward along the coast, stopping first at Sidon. The centurion allowed Paul unusual liberty to visit friends ashore. Putting to sea again, the ship kept to the east and then to the north of Cyprus to gain some shelter[5] from the prevailing westerly winds. By sailing along the mainland coast, the ship was able to take advantage of the land winds, together with the current which runs to the west.[6] By this means the ship made its way along Cilicia and Pamphylia and put in at Myra, a city in Lycia.

Just as the centurion had hoped, he was able to locate a large Rome-bound vessel at Myra. It was an Egyptian grain ship (27:6, 38), one of many which plied the Mediterranean and brought foodstuffs to Italy. The winds being westerly, it was with difficulty (probably by tacking) and very slowly that the ship made its way west to a point opposite Cnidus (see Fig. 23). At Cnidus, however, the ship would lose the advantage of the westerly current, smooth water, and land winds,[7] and her only course was to head south before the northwest wind, and sail under the shelter of Crete. Therefore, the ship sailed around Cape Salmone on the east side of Crete and put in at the harbor of Fair Havens, near the city of Lasea.

B. *The Storm* (27:9-26)

It was now late in the sailing season, for already the Day of

---

[4]*St. Paul the Traveller*, p. 316.

[5]To "sail under" (*hupopleō*) means to sail on the leeward side, or under the shelter of.

[6]James Smith, *The Voyage and Shipwreck of St. Paul* (London, 1856), pp. 63-67.

[7]*Ibid.*, pp. 74, 75.

Atonement was past.[8] Among the ancients the dangerous season for sailing was defined as September 14 to November 11, after which all navigation on the open sea was discontinued.[9] A meeting was called by the centurion to decide whether the ship should stay at Fair Havens for the winter or attempt to reach a more commodious port. Because the ship was part of the government's grain fleet, the centurion actually was the highest authority on board, outranking even the shipowner and the pilot. In spite of Paul's experience as a traveller (which must have been respected inasmuch as he was invited to this planning meeting), his advice to remain at Fair Havens was not followed. Instead it was decided to sail to another harbor of Crete farther to the west.

The goal in view was Phoenix, a harbor probably to be identified with Phineka, a few miles west of Lutro. Although Smith and Ramsay identified Phoenix with Lutro,[10] its harbor faces east, and this hardly fits Luke's description of Phoenix as "looking down the southwest wind and down the northwest wind."[11] As the ship set sail under a light south wind, hopes were high that the goal might be reached.

Before long, however, a violent northeaster (Euraquilo)[12] roared down upon the ship from the mountains of Crete. The violent wind was so strong that the ship could not hold its course, and the vessel was driven southward till it reached the shelter of Cauda,[13] an island about twenty-three miles from Fair Havens. With great effort the ship's dinghy, which was being towed astern, was brought on board. By this time it must have been filled with water and was in danger of being lost. The crew also passed cables under the hull of the ship, drawing them tight to prevent the heaving vessel from breaking apart. Fearing that the ship might be driven onto the sandbars off the

---

[8]The "Fast" (27:9) refers to this annual celebration, which occurred in A.D. 59 on October 5.

[9]Ramsay, *St. Paul the Traveller*, p. 322.

[10]Smith, *Voyage*, p. 86; Ramsay, *St. Paul the Traveller*, p. 326 (Ramsay suggests that since Luke never saw the harbor, he may have misunderstood the sailors).

[11]Greek: *bleponta kata liba kai kata chōron* (27:12).

[12]The term refers to a wind coming from E.N.E.

[13]An alternate reading in some manuscripts is "Clauda."

coast of North Africa known as The Syrtis, the crew lowered the gear[14] so as to slow the ship.

The following day the crew began lightening the ship of non-essentials, and the third day some of the fittings of the vessel itself were jettisoned. The situation had become desperate, and even the crewmen gradually abandoned hope of survival. It was then that Paul came forward with a much-needed word of encouragement. Very humanly he mentioned that his previous advice should have been followed. Even so, he said, he had a fresh message from God assuring him that he would live to stand before Caesar, and that all of his fellow passengers would be spared as well. Paul appears in this narrative as a most unusual prisoner — advising, encouraging, and receiving divine enlightenment. God's remarkable dealings with him on this voyage are doubtless one of the important reasons why Luke has recorded this sea voyage in such detail.

C. *The Shipwreck* (27:27-44)

The hapless ship was being driven by the storm across the Sea of Adria. This name was given to the portion of the Mediterranean between Malta, Italy, Greece, and Crete.[15] At midnight on the fourteenth night the sailors detected signs that they were nearing land, perhaps by hearing the crash of breakers upon the shore. Their fears were confirmed after they had taken several soundings and found the depth to be rapidly decreasing. Immediately the sailors cast four anchors from the stern[16] and hoped fervently for daybreak so that they could make visual observation of their predicament.

A new danger developed when the sailors devised a plot to abandon ship by taking the dinghy. They pretended to be laying out other anchors from the bow (a reasonable procedure), but were actually trying to flee in the only lifeboat. Paul's alertness

---

[14]The text does not state in 27:17 whether what was lowered was the topsail, or a sea anchor, or all the rigging gear which was useless in a storm.

[15]Ramsay, *St. Paul the Traveller,* p. 334. It is not the same as the modern Adriatic Sea between Italy, Yugoslavia, and Albania.

[16]Normally anchors were placed from the bow, but in a violent gale such procedure would be useless for the ship would have immediately swung around. It was important to keep the bow heading toward the land in order to attempt to beach the ship the next morning.

uncovered the scheme, and he warned that the shipboard skills of the sailors would surely be needed in the morning if the total group were to survive. Whether the centurion was wise in cutting loose the dinghy and losing it entirely may be questioned (it could have been useful in effecting the rescue of all the passengers), but he did achieve his purpose of keeping the sailors on board!

Verses 24 and 31 provide an interesting illustration of the Biblical viewpoint regarding divine sovereignty and human responsibility. God knew that all on the vessel would be preserved (and if God knows it, it is certain and cannot be otherwise). At the same time God's sovereignty which insured their safety was not intended to discourage human effort, for this was the means by which God would achieve the end in view.

Again Paul asserted his moral leadership by encouraging the passengers to eat. He set an example by thanking God for the food and then partaking himself, and the rest followed. All 276 persons[17] were strengthened for the remaining tasks that faced them on the ship and in the ordeal of getting to land. The rest of the night was spent in throwing overboard the cargo of wheat so that the ship would ride higher in the water. This would enable the crew to beach it nearer shore when daylight came.

At dawn the sailors did not recognize their whereabouts, but did perceive an inlet with a sandy beach. The careful researches of James Smith in his definitive work *The Voyage and Shipwreck of St. Paul* (London, second edition, 1856) have made it almost certain that the spot was the site now called St. Paul's Bay on the coast of Malta. He used for his calculations the wind direction (E.N.E.) and the average rate of drift of a large sailing ship on a starboard tack[18] (approximately 1½ m.p.h.).

> Hence, according to these calculations, a ship, starting late in the evening from Clauda, would, by midnight on the 14th, be less than three miles from the entrance of St. Paul's Bay. . . . there is no other place agreeing, either in name or description, within the limits to which we are tied down by calculations founded upon the narrative.[19]

---

[17]A few manuscripts (including B) say 76 instead of 276. However, the larger figure is no problem, for many Alexandrian grain ships were very large. Josephus was himself shipwrecked on a vessel that carried 600 (*Life,* 3).

[18]With its right side to the wind.

[19]Pp. 120-124.

Hoping to ground the ship on the beach, the sailors let stern anchors fall into the sea. They loosed the ropes which had held the two rudders immobile, for now they would need to steer as much as possible. They also hoisted the foresail to provide additional steering capability. The ship, however, ran aground upon a reef,[20] with the prow stuck fast, and the stern exposed to the battering force of the waves. The soldiers wanted to kill the prisoners to avoid trouble later if they should escape (see 16:27; 12:19), but the centurion did not so quickly forget the debt owed to Paul. He ordered that everyone should get to shore as best he could, and thus by swimming or by grasping anything that floated, each one made it safety to land.

II. THE WINTER IN MALTA (28:1-10)

A. *Paul's Protection from the Snakebite* (28:1-6)

It was only after reaching the safety of the land that the shipwreck victims learned they were on Malta. Although many of the sailors may have seen or even visited the island before on their way to Rome, none had been at this spot where the wreck occurred. The usual harbor was Valletta.

The natives[21] of Malta welcomed their 276 visitors with great kindness. They first kindled a fire to warm and dry the drenched and bedraggled voyagers. Even though the violence of the storm (at least, the gale force winds) seems to have ended, the rain continued, and the weather had turned cold. Paul continued to demonstrate his helpful spirit by joining in the collecting of firewood. The prisoners had been released in order to make their way to shore, and Paul apparently had not been confined immediately upon landing. This was characteristic of the centurion's treatment of his illustrious prisoner throughout the voyage (27:3, 43).

---

[20]Greek: *topon dithalasson,* "a place of two seas," apparently a reef or shoal.

[21]Greek: *hoi barbaroi* (28:2). The basic meaning of the term denotes the uttering of unintelligible sounds. It developed the meaning of alien, non-Greek people who spoke a different language from Greek. Here it denotes the Maltese, who spoke their native tongue Punic, See Hans Windisch, "Barbaros," *TDNT,* I, 546-553.

During Paul's tending to the fire a viper[22] was disturbed by the increasing heat and fastened itself on his hand (see Mark 16:18). The islanders recognized its bite as poisonous and concluded that Justice[23] must be determined to rid the world of this prisoner, even though he had escaped death in the shipwreck. When Paul shook off the snake and no after-effects occurred (though carefully awaited by the natives), the populace changed its attitude and decided Paul must be a god. Luke has previously recorded a similar change of opinion in reverse (14:11-12, 19), a reminder of the fickleness of human opinion whether good or bad.

B. *The Healing of Publius' Father* (28:7-10)

In the vicinity of the shipwreck site was the estate of Publius, called here "the chief man of the island."[24] In all likelihood "chief" was an official title, for the word has been found with this sense in two inscriptions from Malta.[25] (If he were not an official, it is difficult to see by what criteria Luke would have called him *the* chief man.) He graciously received the large group as his guests for three days until more permanent quarters could be arranged for the winter.

The kind treatment of the travellers by Publius brought an unexpected dividend to him in return. His father had become ill with recurrent fever[26] and dysentery. The physician Luke was present for an accurate diagnosis. Paul, however, prayed for the man and laid hands upon him, and God brought miraculous healing. When the news of his healing circulated through the island, many others who were ailing came to Paul and likewise experienced the removal of their diseases. Throughout their stay on Malta, the travellers, who had lost all their possessions in the shipwreck, experienced continual acts of hospitality from

---

[22]The absence of snakes on Malta today has been viewed as a problem. However, the progress of civilization on the island after 19 centuries can easily account for their complete extermination.

[23]Greek: *hē dikē* (28:4). The expression is used here either in the sense of a goddess, or as a personification of Divine Justice.

[24]Greek: *tōi prōtōi tēs nēsou.*

[25]Jackson and Lake, *The Acts of the Apostles*, IV, 342.

[26]Greek: *puretois,* a plural form.

the islanders. Luke's entire book has shown that virtually everyone was friendly to Paul except his own countrymen.

III. THE ARRIVAL IN ROME (28:11-31)

A. *The Final Journey* (28:11-16)

After spending the three winter months in Malta while ship-
ping lanes were closed, the Rome-bound company finally set
sail in a ship from Alexandria which had wintered at Malta.
This was the third ship utilized on the voyage, and the second
from Alexandria (27:2, 6). It may also have been one of the
grain ships in state service. The ship bore the figurehead of the
Twin Brothers,[27] Castor and Pollux. These mythological figures
were revered by sailors, and their constellation Gemini was supposed to bring good luck in a storm.[28]

The ship made its way first to Syracuse on the island of Sicily,
a distance of about 80 miles. After a three-day layover the vessel
made its way 70 miles to Rhegium, a port at the toe of Italy
along the Strait of Messina. When a south wind rose, the ship
made the 180 miles to Puteoli in just two days. Puteoli was located by the Bay of Naples, and was the regular port for the
Alexandrian grain fleet. Here Paul came in contact with some
Christian brethren[29] who invited him to be their guest for a
week. Apparently the centurion had other reasons for delaying
his journey to Rome, so that Paul was able to accept this kind
invitation from these Christians. Doubtless a soldier accompanied
Paul at all times (28:16).

On the final stages of the overland journey, some Christians
came from Rome to greet Paul. One company came thirty-three
miles south of Rome to Three Inns,[30] another came ten miles
farther to Appius Forum, located on the Appian Way, the famous road leading from Rome across the south of Italy. Although Paul had never been to Rome, he had many friends
there already and these were organized into churches which met

---

[27]Greek: *Dioskourois* ("Sons of Zeus").

[28]Jackson and Lake, *The Acts of the Apostles*, IV, 343.

[29]It is assumed that the "brethren" in 28:14 and 15 were Christians, in
distinction from the "Jews" of 28:17 and 23.

[30]Greek: *Trion Tabernon.*

in various homes (Rom. 16:3-16, esp. vss. 5, 14, 15).[31] Two of these groups came to welcome Paul to their city, in fulfillment of his wish expressed at least three years before (Rom. 15:24).

At last the city itself was entered. Julius the centurion delivered his prisoners into other hands, and Paul was allowed the courtesy of separate confinement, guarded only by one soldier assigned to him for this purpose.

B. Paul's Activity in Rome (28:17-31)

1. Interview with Jewish Leaders (28:17-22)

After Paul had gotten settled in Rome, he made contact with the leaders of the Jewish community and invited them to his quarters. He still retained his love for his nation, and hoped that he could pursue his same policy as in other cities of reaching the Jews first with the gospel before that door should be closed to him.

When the leaders came, Paul explained that his imprisonment, even though caused by Jewish agitation against him, did not imply that he had any bad feelings against Jewish customs or the Jewish people. The light chain[32] or handcuff which he wore was actually caused by Paul's dedication to the Messianic hope of Israel, for it was the proclamation of the claims of the resurrected Jesus as Israel's Messiah that had aroused the hatred of many Jews and had brought about his arrest.

The Roman Jews responded that they had heard nothing from Judea about Paul's case, although they were aware of the Christian movement, that it was being denounced everywhere in their circles. They expressed an interest in hearing Paul's views. Their ignorance of Paul's case is surprising at first thought, and an explanation can be suggested only with hesitancy. If Paul had been sent to Rome very soon after he had appealed, the Palestinian Jews may have been unable to get word to Rome sooner, for Paul himself must have arrived on one of the first ships to reach Italy that spring. It also may be true that the Jews from Palestine had decided not to pursue the case further, inasmuch

---

[31]This conclusion is based upon the view that Romans 16 is a genuine part of the Epistle to the Romans, and was not written to Ephesus as some claim.

[32]This chain was far different from the bindings for the scourge which Lysias had once used (22:25, 29).

Fig. 24. Ruins of the Roman Forum (in Paul's day). Photo by the author

Fig. 25. The Roman Forum (reconstruction)

as they had been unsuccessful with Felix and Festus, and both Festus and Agrippa had pronounced Paul innocent of any crime. Rome sometimes dealt harshly with accusers who failed to substantiate their cases. Likewise, the Jewish community in Rome may not have wished attention drawn to themselves at this time, having only recently been allowed to return to Rome following their earlier banishment by Claudius.[33]

2. A Second Interview with the Jews (28:23-28)[34]

A date was set for a second meeting between Paul and the Jews at which a large number from the Jewish community in Rome were present. An entire day was spent as Paul demonstrated from all portions of the OT (both Law and Prophets) how Jesus was the fulfilment of scriptural prediction, and was the Messiah who would establish the kingdom of God.

The interview was respectful on both sides, and the results were typical of Paul's experiences elsewhere (except for the absence of violence). Some were favorable to his message but others were not. In closing Paul referred to the words of Isaiah 6:9-10 (LXX), a quotation used twice elsewhere in the NT by Jesus (Matt. 13:14-15; Mark 4:12; Luke 8:10) and by John (John 12:40-41). It spoke of Israel's refusal to believe God's message in spite of repeated opportunity and revelation. Paul's unpersuaded hearers were after the same pattern as their fathers seven hundred years earlier. Jewish refusal, however, did not bring God's plan of salvation to ruin, but opened the way for its extension to gentiles directly. No Jew had reason to complain, for he had been given opportunity and had turned it down.

3. Paul's Continuing Ministry (28:30, 31)

The next two years saw Paul in Rome waiting for his appeal to Caesar to be heard. He continued to enjoy considerable freedom to exercise a preaching and teaching ministry, with no hindrance except confinement to his quarters and a chain attaching him to a soldier (28:20).

---

[33]See on 18:2.

[34]Verse 29 is omitted by P[74] Aleph A B E, and is not included in most Greek testaments today. It is found in the Western and Byzantine texts, however.

During this time Paul wrote four of the NT epistles: Ephesians, Philippians,[35] Colossians, and Philemon. He also received many visitors, some of whom are known to us. Tychicus was with Paul in Rome and delivered three of Paul's letters (Eph. 6:21; Col. 4:7-9). Onesimus, the runaway slave, contacted Paul in Rome and was sent back to his master, along with a letter that the church still treasures (Philem. 10; Col. 4:9). Timothy was also in Rome part of the time (Phil. 1:1; Col. 1:1; Philem. 1). Epaphroditus brought a gift to Paul from the Philippians (Phil. 4:18). Epaphras came from Colosse with a report from the church there (Col. 1:7, 8). Others with him at various times were Mark (Col. 4:10), Jesus Justus (Col. 4:11), and Demas (Col. 4:14), as well as Luke (Col. 4:14) and Aristarchus (Col. 4:10) who had come originally on the voyage.

What happened when Paul's case was finally heard? Luke does not say, and the reason may be that it had not been decided when he wrote his fascinating account to Theophilus. However, the author has given every indication for his readers to suppose that eventually the illustrious prisoner would be set free. There are good reasons for concluding that when the apostle was released, he resumed his missionary travels, perhaps visited Spain (Rom. 15:24), and wrote the Pastoral Epistles, the final letters we possess from his pen.[36] At a second imprisonment in Rome some years later, he laid down his life, having "finished the course" and "kept the faith" (II Tim. 4:7).

Thus Luke brought to an end his absorbing account of the most dramatic thirty years of Christian history. From the beginnings in Jerusalem with a little band of disciples in an upper room, he has sketched with sure and steady strokes the advance of the church across the land of its birth to the very capital of the Roman world. Neither persecution from the state, nor occasional unfaithfulness within its own ranks, could stop its relentless march. The reason, of course, was that the risen Christ was working by his Spirit within the believers, accomplishing the goals that he had laid before them (1:8). The challenge remains for the modern reader to place his faith likewise in Jesus Christ,

---

[35]Some place the writing of Philippians earlier at Ephesus, but the traditional view has not been seriously undermined.

[36]See Kent, *The Pastoral Epistles,* pp. 42-53.

and become a part of this incomparable enterprise which Acts so graphically describes. The same Jesus and the same Spirit are still accomplishing the purposes of God in the lives of men.

QUESTIONS FOR DISCUSSION

1. Why did Luke devote so much space to his description of the voyage?
2. In what ways did the centurion Julius show unusual respect for Paul? Why do you think he did this?
3. If Paul knew that *all* on the ship would be safe, why did he say that the sailors must remain on board to insure the safety of the others?
4. Why doesn't Acts state the outcome of Paul's case? What do you think happened?

BIBLIOGRAPHY

Aharoni, Yohanan, and Michael Avi-Yonah. *The Macmillan Bible Atlas.* New York: The Macmillan Company, 1968.

Alexander, Joseph Addison. *Commentary on the Acts of the Apostles.* Grand Rapids: Zondervan Publishing House, reprinted 1956.

Alford, Henry. *The New Testament for English Readers.* Chicago: Moody Press, n. d.

Ante-Nicene Fathers, ed. Alexander Roberts and James Donaldson. Grand Rapids: Wm. B. Eerdmans Publishing Co., 1951.

Arndt, William F., and F. Wilbur Gingrich. *A Greek-English Lexicon of the New Testament.* Chicago: University of Chicago Press, 1957.

Aune, David E. "The Text Tradition of Luke-Acts," *Bulletin of the Evangelical Theological Society,* Vol. 7, No. 3 (Summer, 1964).

Babylonian Talmud, trans. Michael L. Rodkinson. Boston: The Talmud Society, 1918.

Bernard, L. W. "St. Stephen and Alexandrian Christianity," *New Testament Studies,* Vol. 7, No. 1 (October, 1960).

Biblia Hebraica, ed. Rud. Kittel. Stuttgart: Privileg. Wurtt. Bibelanstalt, reprinted 1954.

The Biblical World, ed. Charles F. Pfeiffer. Grand Rapids: Baker Book House, 1966.

Blaiklock, E. M. *The Acts of the Apostles* in The Tyndale New Testament Commentaries. Grand Rapids: Wm. B. Eerdmans Publishing Co., 1959.

Boyer, James L. *New Testament Chronological Chart.* Winona Lake, Indiana: James L. Boyer, 1962.

Broneer, Oscar. "Paul and the Pagan Cults," *Harvard Theological Review,* Vol. 64, Nos. 2, 3 (April, July, 1971).

Bruce, F. F. *The Acts of the Apostles, The Greek Text with Introduction and Commentary.* Grand Rapids: Wm. B. Eerdmans Publishing Co., reprinted 1968.

_____. *The Book of the Acts* in The New International Commentary on the New Testament. Grand Rapids: Wm. B. Eerdmans Publishing Co., 1954.

Cadbury, H. J. "Acts of the Apostles," *The Interpreter's Dictionary of the Bible.* New York: Abingdon Press, 1962.

Calvin, John. *Commentaries on the Epistles of Paul to the Galatians and Ephesians,* trans. William Pringle. Grand Rapids: Wm. B. Eerdmans Publishing Co., reprinted 1948.

Chafer, Lewis Sperry. *Systematic Theology.* Dallas: Dallas Seminary Press, 1948.

Conybeare, W. J., and J. W. Howson. *The Life and Epistles of St. Paul.* Grand Rapids: Wm. B. Eerdmans Publishing Co., reprinted 1951.

Cousins, Peter. "Stephen and Paul," *The Evangelical Quarterly,* Vol. XXXIII, No. 3 (July, 1961).

Currie, Stuart D. "Speaking in Tongues," *Interpretation,* Vol. XIX, No. 3 (July, 1965).

Deissman, G. Adolf. *Bible Studies.* Edinburgh: T. & T. Clark, 1901.

Eusebius Pamphili, *Ecclesiastical History.* Translated by Roy J. Deferrari in The Fathers of the Church. Washington, D.C.: The Catholic University of America Press, 1953.

Everyday Life in Bible Times, ed. Melville Bell Grosvenor and Frederick G. Vosburgh. National Geographic Society, 1967.

Finegan, Jack. *The Archaeology of the New Testament.* Princeton University Press, 1969.

Foakes Jackson, F. J. *The Acts of the Apostles* in The Moffatt New Testament. Commentary. London: Hodder and Stoughton, Ltd., 1960.

Foakes Jackson, F. J., and Kirsopp Lake. *The Acts of the Apostles.* Part I of The Beginnings of Christianity, Volumes IV and V. Grand Rapids: Baker Book House, reprinted 1965.

Gasque, W. W. "The Historical Value of the Book of Acts," *The Evangelical Quarterly.* Vol. XLI, No. 2 (April, 1969).

Gerstner, John. "Acts," *The Biblical Expositor.* Philadelphia: A. J. Holman Co., 1960.

Glover, Richard. " 'Luke the Antiochene' and Acts," *New Testament Studies,* Vol. 11, No. 1 (October, 1964).

Grant, F. W. *The Numerical Bible.* New York: Loizeaux Brothers, n.d.

Greece and Rome, Builders of Our World, ed. Melville Bell Grosvenor. National Geographic Society, 1968.

The Greek New Testament, ed. Kurt Aland, Matthew Black, Bruce M. Metzger, Allen Wikgren. London: United Bible Societies, 1966.

Grollenberg, L. H. *Atlas of the Bible.* New York: Thomas Nelson and Sons, 1956.

Guthrie, Donald. *New Testament Introduction, The Gospels and Acts.* Chicago: Inter-Varsity, 1965.

Hadas, Moses. *Imperial Rome.* New York: Time Incorporated, 1965.

Harrison, Everett F. *Introduction to the New Testament.* Grand Rapids: Wm. B. Eerdmans Publishing Co., 1964.

Hē Kainē Diathēkē, ed. G. D. Kilpatrick. London: The British and Foreign Bible Society, second edition, 1968.

Hitchcock, R. D., and Francis Brown. *Teaching of the Twelve Apostles.* New York: Charles Scribner's Sons, 1885.

Hobart, William Kirk. *The Medical Language of St. Luke.* Grand Rapids: Baker Book House, reprinted 1954.

Hoehner, Harold W. "The Duration of the Egyptian Bondage," *Bibliotheca Sacra.* Vol. 126, No. 504 (October, 1969).

Ironside, H. A. *Lectures on the Book of Acts.* New York: Loizeaux Brothers, 1943.

Josephus, *Jewish Antiquities,* trans. H. St. J. Thackeray, in The Loeb Classical Library. Cambridge: Harvard University Press, 1957.

--------. *The Jewish War,* trans. H. St. J. Thackery, in The Loeb Classical Library. Cambridge: Harvard University Press, 1956.

————. *The Life*, trans. H. St. J. Thackeray, in The Loeb Classical Library. Cambridge: Harvard University Press, 1956.

Justin Martyr, "First Apology." *The Fathers of the Church*. Washington, D.C.; The Catholic University of America Press, 1965.

Kent, Homer A., Jr. *The Pastoral Epistles*. Chicago: Moody Press, 1958.

————. "Paul Departed from Athens and Came to Corinth," *The Brethren Misionary Herald*. Vol. 31, No. 26 (December 27, 1969).

Klijn, A. F. J. "Stephen's Speech," *New Testament Studies*, Vol. IV, No. 1 (October, 1957).

Knowling, R. J. "The Acts of the Apostles," *The Expositor's Greek Testament*, ed. W. Robertson Nicoll. Volume II. Grand Rapids: Wm. B. Eerdmans Publishing Co., reprint edition.

Lenski, R. C. H. *Interpretation of the Acts of the Apostles*. Columbus: The Wartburg Press, 1944.

Lightfoot, J. B. *The Apostolic Fathers*. London: Macmillan and Co., 1889.

————. *The Epistle of St. Paul to the Galatians*. Grand Rapids: Zondervan Publishing House, reprint edition.

Lumby, J. Rawson. *The Acts of the Apostles* in The Cambridge Greek Testament for Schools and Colleges. Cambridge University Press, 1885.

Macgregor, G. H. C., and Theodore P. Ferris. "The Acts of the Apostles," *The Interpreter's Bible*, ed. George A. Buttrick. New York: Abingdon-Cokesbury Press, 1954.

Machen, J. Graham. *The Origin of Paul's Religion*. Grand Rapids: Wm. B. Eerdmans Publishing Co., reprinted 1947.

Manson, T. W. *Studies in the Gospels and Epistles*, ed. Matthew Black. Philadelphia: The Westminster Press, 1962.

McCown, C. C. "The Density of Population in Ancient Palestine," *Journal of Biblical Literature*. Vol. 66, Part 4 (December, 1947).

Meyer, H. A. W. *Handbook to the Epistle to the Galatians*. New York: Funk & Wagnalls, Publishers, 1884.

Morgan, G. Campbell. *The Acts of the Apostles*. New York: Fleming H. Revell Co., 13th edition, 1924.

Moulton, W. F., and A. S. Geden. *A Concordance to the Greek Testament*. Edinburgh: T. & T. Clark, 1950.

Munck, Johannes. *The Acts of the Apostles* in The Anchor Bible. Garden City: Doubleday & Company, Inc., 1967.

New Bible Commentary, ed. F. Davidson. Grand Rapids: Wm. B. Eerdmans Publishing Co., 1958.

New Bible Dictionary, ed. J. D. Douglas. Grand Rapids: Wm. B. Eerdmans Publishing Co., 1962.

Novum Testamentum Graece, ed. Eberhard Nestle, Erwin Nestle, and Kurt Aland, 25th edition. Stuttgart: Wurttembergische Bibelanstalt, 1963.

Orr, Robert W. "Paul's Voyage and Shipwreck," *The Evangelical Quarterly*, Vol XXXV, No. 2 (April, 1963).

Perowne, Stewart. *The Later Herods*. New York: Abingdon Press, 1958.

————. *The Life and Times of Herod the Great*. New York: Abingdon Press, n. d.

Pfeiffer, Charles F., and Howard F. Vos. *The Wycliffe Historical Geography of Bible Lands.* Chicago: Moody Press, 1967.

Rackham, Richard B. *The Acts of the Apostles.* London: Methuen & Co., Ltd., 14th edition, 1951.

Ramsay, William M. *The Bearing of Recent Discovery on the Trustworthiness of the New Testament.* Grand Rapids: Baker Book House, reprinted 1953.

————. *The Cities of St. Paul.* Grand Rapids: Baker Book House, reprinted 1949.

————. *St. Paul the Traveller and the Roman Citizen.* Grand Rapids: Baker Book House, reprinted 1949.

Riggs, Jack R. "The Length of Israel's Sojourn in Egypt," *Grace Journal.* Vol. 12, No. 1 (Winter, 1971).

Septuaginta, ed. Alfred Rahlfs. Stuttgart: Privileg. Wurtt. Bibelanstalt, 1950.

Smith, Charles R. "Biblical Conclusions Concerning Tongues." Unpublished doctoral dissertation, Grace Theological Seminary, 1970.

Smith, James. *The Voyage and Shipwreck of St. Paul,* second edition. London: Longman, Brown, Green, Longmans, & Roberts, 1856.

Sokolowski, F. "A New Testimony on the Cult of Artemis of Ephesus," *Harvard Theological Review,* Vol. 58, No. 4 (October, 1965).

Suetonius, *The Twelve Caesars,* trans. Robert Graves (Penguin Books). London: Whitefriars Press Ltd., 1957.

"A Symposium on the Tongues Movement," *Bibliotheca Sacra.* Vol. 120, No. 480 (October, 1963).

Tacitus, *The Annals and The Histories,* trans. Alfred John Church and William Jackson Brodribb, in Great Books of the Western World, ed. Robert Maynard Hutchens. Vol. 15. U.S.A.: Encyclopaedia Brittannica, Inc., 1952.

Theological Dictionary of the New Testament, ed. Gerhard Kittel, trans. Geoffrey W. Bromiley. Grand Rapids: Wm. B. Eerdmans Publishing Co., 1964-1968.

Toussaint, Stanley D. "The Chronological Problems of Galatians 2:1-10," *Bibliotheca Sacra, Vol.* 120, No. 480 (October, 1963).

Unger, Merrill F. "Archaeology and Paul's Campaign at Philippi," *Bibliotheca Sacra,* Vol. 119, No. 474 (April, 1962).

————. "Archaeology and Paul's Tour of Cyprus," *Bibliotheca Sacra,* Vol. 117, No. 467 (July, 1960).

————. "Archaeology and Paul's Visit to Iconium, Lystra, and Derbe," *Bibliotheca Sacra,* Vol. 118, No. 470 (April, 1961.

————. "Historical Research and the Church at Thessalonica," *Bibliotheca Sacra,* Vol. 119, No. 473 (January, 1962).

————. "Pisidian Antioch and Gospel Penetration of the Greek World," *Bibliotheca Sacra,* Vol. 118, No. 469 (January, 1961).

Walton, Arthur B. "Stephen's Speech." Unpublished doctoral dissertation, Grace Theological Seminary, 1972.

The Westminster Historical Atlas to the Bible, ed. George Ernest Wright and Floyd Vivian Filson. Philadelphia: The Westminster Press, revised 1956.

Whitcomb, John C., Jr. *Chart of Old Testament Patriarchs and Judges.* Chicago: Moody Press, 1968.

Wright, George Ernest. *Biblical Archaeology.* Philadelphia: The Westminster Press, 1962.

Zimmerman, Charles. "To This Agree the Words of the Prophets," *Grace Journal,* Vol. 4, No. 3 (Fall, 1963).

Zondervan Pictorial Bible Dictionary, The, ed. Merrill C. Tenney. Grand Rapids: Zondervan Publishing House, revised 1967.